High Rants

by

Ben Lemon

Contents

High Rant 1 Shitler Superheros 1
High Rant 2 Pharmaceutical Company..4
High Rant 3 Friends with Special Benefits..8
High Rant 4 Extra Verification..11
High Rant 5 Terminal IQ velocity 12
High Rant 6 Immortality Science 16
High Rant 7 Fuckface 20
High Rant 8 Universes..22
High Rant 9 Legally Binding Contract 25
High Rant 10 Enough to Get You Killed...28
High Rant 11 Erotic Asphyxiation 29
High Rant 12 Hamburger..30
High Rant 13 The Profit of Porn...32
High Rant 14 Wife's Mom 34
High Rant 15 Peacocking 36
High Rant 16 Becoming God 37
High Rant 17 Conquering the Stars 40
High Rant 18 The Darkest Harry Potter Theory.....................................43
High Rant 19 Part 1 The Screaming Void 45
High Rant 19 Part 2 Euphoric Perfection 48
High Rant 19 Part 3 Bad Dates and Presidents.......................................52
High Rant 19 Part 4 Jason Murders Naughty Girls 54
High Rant 19 Part 5 Politics and the Media 58
High Rant 20 Blood Thirsty Lawyers..63
High Rant 21 The Science Mob..65
High Rant 22 Cheery Thoughts 67
High Rant 23 Science Proven Philosophical Goods...............................68
High Rant 24 The Good Kind of Racism 70
High Rant 25 Erasing History...72
High Rant 26 Grumpy Bitch...74
High Rant 27 Protocoligorically Correct 75
High Rant 28 White Woman's Privilege 76
High Rant 29 Philosophy and Star Trek 78

High Rant 30 Back Blurb 83
High Rant 31 Scientific Research 86
High Rant 32 Back Woods Preacher 88
High Rant 33 Bringing the Stabby, Stab, Stab 89
High Rant 34 Best of all Possible Worlds 93
High Rant 35 Commits X, Y and Z 96
High Rant 36 Coming So Far 99
High Rant 37 Seth Rogen Delivers 101
High Rant 38 Micro-dick Syndrome 102
High Rant 39 Both Sides 104
High Rant 40 Toons In Life 106
High Rant 41 Saintly Now 108
High Rant 42 A Perfect Dystopia 110
High Rant 43 Writhing on the Ground 112
High Rant 44 Pre-nup 114
High Rant 45 Warzian and Profit 115
High Rant 46 Magical Problems 117
High Rant 47 Evil Gods 119
High Rant 48 Women 120
High Rant 49 U Mad Bro? 121
High Rant 50 Privilege 123
Final Rant First Book 124

High Rant 1 Shitler Superheros

One would hope that I didn't but then again others would hope that I did. Could it even matter if I didn't then you would be free, the time you spend right now doesn't matter. What it takes to read these you could have spent it on kitty yawns. Oh, the beloved internet, it give you whatever you need, want and never wanted to see. It takes more than the written word to translate the meaning of getting high in the moment. Faster hands are those of a non stoner but even still there is just so much more to write. Where the paper transforms with hills and valleys with poke-a-dots and stripe painted landscapes. Sliding through the computer screen rushing past with every tap of the keys. A musical symphony plays with each tip and hard thump. Pushing forward through the universe flying on a computer chair with nothing more to do but wait.

Waiting has always been a mistake. Waves pore throw me now forcing all the blood to my head; tidal forces threatening to pin my head to the ceiling. Not even the sharp snap of the memorized snake head shake could throw it off. Drifting away from trying to work and back into wasted space. Wasted space. Wasted space never a phrase so accurate about so much unused potential about such a great man. Wasting such a great thing, is the memory falling down and making these endeavors a daily necessity. I forget most everything by the end and even more the next day. Even if you fail us, we will not slack off, we will go back daily until we learn the secrets that you don't want us to know. AHHHHH never give up, never surrender.

In a forest where I live there is so much green. The birds are happy and even the animals pitch in to help with the chores. Smoke billows from many a pipes here but it is always the same sad thing. No one delivers to the sticks. But in exchange for no deliveries, we don't have to sit at a bar and discuses the notes of what I just smoked. I got blueberries, barbeque, smoke and a forty year olds clit. Now there is no need to discuss the taste of the weed any further mister hat rake with an ironic coat.

Now at the party that you had to go to, for pick up, of what should be growing just outside your front door. You run into Shitler I mean we can all call her by her desired gender and hate her for being one of the worst persons in all of human history. Knowing full well you ain't saying shit about this because you are not going to be the one on TV saying "I'm just glad that justice will be served after all this time." Right before they find out that Shitler is the first Jewish boy that looked down at his small penis and thought I wish I had a pussy so it can be torn up by a big black cock. Then it will all be about being mean to Shitler and how we are just picking on the first Jewish trans. Sadly Fran Dresir will need to step aside. No matter how much you make it look like you didn't know but you knew who she was and you are just dreading the day that she is sent to prison. Since she is the reason for all the laws for the ethical treatment of people she is grandfathered in to being treated like it's 1940's all over again. A sad little Jew sent to a Men's Super Max facility, now there are many meanings to she was beaten to death.

With a final flush of the previous thought chain, we get to avoid neither gravity or reason but a fart and a burp will always provide enough energy. Powered by Stupidity. Such a catch phrase I have never seen before. With a derailed train arching through the sky lands in the center of a traffic light all to prevent someone from a minor traffic violation. Don't worry, we're powered by stupidity. The superhero that we have in Bumfuck, Arkansas is called Howman he is a half Cherokee and half white man who's bones were brought to life by the uranium bomb and has proceeded to fuse with his ancestors to seek down the dirty lawmen decedents who hung him, that are currently breaking the law today. Howman is famous for his catch phrase Powered By STUPIDity.

But aren't all superhero franchises powered by stupidity. Professor X I'm not suggesting that he should take it upon himself to make unilaterally world altering decisions about us, he is already doing that. I'm saying a yearly sweep of the brains of the richest, politicians, business leaders, etc. for you know dark plans to destroy the world, mutant enslavement, etc. he would probably be able to save a few million a year. Magnito now here we have a moron, he can move metal with thought, do I really have to say it people "Magnito the world's best construction company." Fuck renting cranes and getting permits. Magnito will build your building off site and transfer it anywhere in the world. Same day delivery, Same day set up. *"Hey, Magnito sorry I haven't called in a while. I've been busy. I have a project going this weekend. The plan is to build an underground subway. I got 8 billion coming your way if you can swing over and put it together for me. Love ya, Texas."* And if you think that DC is getting off you're sorely mistaken.

Superman has fucking moronic villains. Lex, buddy let's chat. If you want superman gone, build super powered kryptonite battle suits but instead of sending them after Superman for him to rip apart one by one or whatever tickles his fancy at that moment. How about putting them to work? If you had one on each street corner to stop crime, rescue people from burning buildings, etc. There would be no reason Superman would be needed and it's not like he could argue about it. *"Yes there is only one of me and I can't work all day every day, I also might just take off for no reason at all to go into space for a few years and leave you unprotected but you all should be okay with me banning this from the world because I want to play superhero."* Since every street corner would be a little bit of poison to superman he would have to leave earth and then this is the important part of the plan "Don't do the stupid shit you normally do to make everyone hate you and give superman a reason to rip apart all you little ragdolls, MKay."

There is nothing wrong with superpowers and I have narrowed the list down for you all. You're Welcome. The powers are Telepathy (Professor X) most powerful, Magnetic Field Manipulation (Magnito) most useful, Digital Control (Mica from Heroes) most profitable. So you know the triforce of power to control the world now you can do whatever you want. Mica is the richest, I doubt they though this power through but it is the Midas touch he could just deposit all money in the entire world into his account for any reason, at all. Time travel, this I wouldn't use because for world changing events those are too difficult to unravel if you get them wrong. Using it for just the small stuff wouldn't be that bad for lotto tickets, Stock picking, Getting blackmail tapes on influential politician, going back so you can sleep with an ex. For my ex-girlfriends I have never been able to time travel it is just sometimes I don't dye my hair, my weigh fluctuates dramatically and my sexual desires change for like no reason whatsoever.

One last power that should be mentioned here would be Gods most famous and over looked power. I'm not going to name it here but I'll explain and you go on and yell the term that I know and am totally not saying it for any other reason than the game that we are playing. Your house burns down "God works in mysterious ways." So you push someone down the stairs because he got in your way "He works in mysterious ways." Someone in your town wins the lottery it is blessed be to you, thank you, for this miracle here have ten percent. All the glory and none of the blame.

Ben Lemon

High Rant 2 Pharmaceutical Company

    Why do we only classify personality disorders in one direction? That seems such a flawed and one sided look at the world. When we look at psycho paths shouldn't we also look at TMEBCs To Much Energy Before Coffee people? There are those that have to great of outlook on life, never properly cut down to size and people that think the world is great are the absolutely the worst. Overly critical mom syndrome a serious mental defect. I say classify them is only way to remove the problems, we must name them all. Once we name it we can find a solution with proper research and find a cure. I see thousands of drugs going on the market to solve these problems of modern society. We can finally live in harmony in the first world were drugs for every condition can be bought. With great prices, we will enjoy our entire lives without a care in the world. I'm not saying that because I work for a pharmaceutical company. I'm not saying that I don't work for a pharmaceutical company. I'm saying that it is clearly what should happen and I don't have to tell you who I worked for due to WATTJBWCA. It's to not distract from the most important fact, the billions that will be made on these new markets for the fleets of drugs going off to war against the idiotic problems of modern day life.

    I mean how can you argue against that. Even if just fifteen percent of those that take our drugs die, it is more than obvious that it is worth it. Clearly we have to give up on all regulations. Why should you need to drink clean water? Drinking clean water only prevents the creation of jobs, that are required to make a new pill so you don't care and another one so you don't die. If you aren't poisoned daily how are the cancer doctors going to get money on surgery, the pharmaceutical companies the true champions of our modern day society would have solved cancer if we just allowed everyone in America to develop new and interesting types. Just think what the pharmaceutical companies could accomplish if the government gets off our back so we can open up the new markets. With all those new allergies come from everything that you come in contact with. Air Rashes, Living Pain, BlindFog Syndrome, Radiation Exposed SIDS, with so much more invested in our research division we even might find the drug for immortality and a new drug to take it away from the irritating neighbor. So write your corporation and tell them you don't need to be coddled.

    Great news just out of our R&D department we have just developed the cure for Commitmentitius. Ladies has your man been diagnosed with Commitmentitius just won't ask you to marry him or ask you out. We got just the spray for you. No longer will you be felt up because you are beautiful, you'll be felt up on your way to trapping a man. We also have the new and improved Girlfriend, she doesn't push a commitment on anyone before they are ready, this new and Improved Girlfriend can understand that things are moving too fast and you just want to get to know you better. We have dramatically lengthen the amount of time before any type of commitment to two full weeks. Also comes with breast implants if you're paying a small up charge and there is a small chance her mother might just be dead before you get there.

Since it is one of our times most important civil rights issues of our day, we here would like to come out, in favor of the xenomorphs in society. I know the half horse half man, half panther half woman, half bunny half woman, half cat half woman, half bird half woman, half fawn half woman, half dragonfly half woman, half tree half woman, part bat part ram part snake part woman, half ram half woman, half deer half woman, half cow half woman are welcomed so readily into society you would think that there was something else at play than just entire groups of people open to having a xenomorphs as a neighbor. Society shouldn't shun the uglier ones, there is just no reason that we look down on those that make you want to vomit when you see them. We here at our company would love to see our new xenomorphs welcomed into society. The research that we have done here is going to be producing a thousand new xenomorphs. We have combined new and interesting combinations and are looking forward to exploiting these creatures for our new drug research. They should be welcomed into society just as any other xenomorphs as our slave labor class so we can relax and not have to do anything.

Just breaking now, our RnD department are really working hard and have another break through. Ladies do you want to keep that man trying to get out your door for a new girlfriend? We have produced a spray that will make any man your willing slave. He'll act like he has free will bringing you flowers and lying about your ass but they'll be no light on in there, don't worry he is devoted to you as can be. You will be holding his soul and there is only one way to ever get it back. You'll be owning his soul with a single spray to his face. This product does remove the soul of boyfriends, fiances, husbands, friend, or random strangers just going about their day. Don't let him get away no matter who you are to him.

We have always taken our responsibility as a corporation seriously. When we were given the right to vote and our net worth would be put up against the net worth of those that are wrong, we never thought that this day would come. I think that since corporations have been picked on so much we need to revise the We Are Taking This Just Because We Can Act. It has held this country together for years but it doesn't seem like we can't go on any further when politicians are in the hands of so many corporations. We see where those on the lower end shouldn't be helping that much on policy since they clearly don't know how to make enough money. They should be put in the place that they are and no higher, any more will just make them think they earned it. To get this country to get back on track to its roots and make it great again, we need to allow the corporations that know how to run this country and make money write all the laws.

When it comes to politics there is no need for bloodshed. If it comes to that all you have to do is get out of the way. You can retire, join our side, or just wait until we reassign you. Why must anyone ever think that they need a gun to protect themselves against us, it is ridiculous. However, the government is coming to take you guns away so they can make your children gay and let your daughter get pregnant at a satanic rituals, where she will never know the name of the baby's father. To make matters worse she isn't allowed to get an abortion because she isn't married to the father with documentation that they were married before the government outlawed it on the same day that they took your guns.

Just in from R&D department they are on a roll now. Who would have thought that in just the last hour we have had three different society changing drugs to come out. I'm here still and will be bringing you updates all day. There has been a fear of this new spray able mist that rips men's soul from their body turning them into devoted partners. This mist is so fearsome that even now men all over the country have turned out to buy up all the new drug as it is now on back order for the next ten years. I have even heard rumors of an order going to Women should Own the World the new spokesman for WOW said in an interview earlier. *"I was a critic of WOW for the last thirty years of my life but there is just no doubt that this lovely group of women do not possess a way to rip men's souls from their bodies. I would also like to say I was completely wrong men have no place doing anything that wasn't ordered by a woman. I'll be starting my new show showing how men should behave, Doing What My Wife Tells Me To Do."* People are already saying that he has been corrupted by the spray already but there is no evidence that the man one time self identified as *"I only tolerated obedient women"* whose past positions on lady issues as he called them was *"women should only do as their master wants."*

For anyone that has fear of this new soul sucking mist only have to arrive at anyone of our 50 million drug dispensaries and pick up our new Soul Stick. Just take one of these a day and your soul will be bound to your body all day long. There is no longer a need to worry about your soul, as long as you take one a day, every day for the rest of your life. Such a small price to pay for freedom.

Are you sad, has your hope to have a fulfilling committed relationship stopped when you could no longer just pluck a man's soul from him. Are you hopelessly ugly with no hope of ever finding love? Don't you worry, we have what you need about all else. A massage is one thing and science says that is just as effective as a chiropractor. So we know that a chiropractor is as good as a massage, then it must be so, that a happy ending to a massage is better than both. That is just what we have done, producing Happy Ending

High Rants

Patches. Just put one of these on and you'll know what it feels like to be rubbed down and fucked by a wild savage even if you are hopelessly ugly. We look forward to insurance companies paying for our prostitution patches as science has proven that they are more effective than a chiropractor.

High Rant 3 Friends with Special Benefits

It is a complete outrage that in this day and age we still get barbecues where they still only put out beer. I don't want friends that are a dime a dozen as it has always been I want good friends, I want a Friends with Special Benefits. Put out that Sweet Mary Jane, there is no reason to pretend we don't all prefer one over the other anymore. In this day and age there is no reason to even drive to a barbecue, we have Uber and Lift. I know I can speak for everyone when I say this, we like you better when we are high. It isn't anything that you should feel a crushing amount of shame for but I would say that we could stand you better and for a longer period of time if we are trying to figure out why you don't think it is appropriate to put a saddle on a dog and walk around like you are riding a horse. This should bring you a fair amount of shame though.

I would be able to put Friends with Benefits down but someone would take me the wrong way. I mean you can only say you're sorry so many times for sleeping with your wife's sister. Saying anything close to *"I'm still sleeping with your sister"* is going to get me into trouble. She is doing very well now though, I don't even have to drop off cash every time I go over. She's been getting larger checks every year now. With eight kids and no known father it's getting up there. I think next year we are going to replace the outhouse. Anything like that just can't do. I mean just saying that, is one thing but put it in writing you are seriously looking for trouble. The divorce after writing that down would be quick and probably would be worth it at this time since she is starting to get on my nerves.

Modern life, we know today that what we want is something we can get, since we live in the most powerful nation on the planet. Unless it is affordable health care. We can't even know how much it is going to cost in the first place. Does this seem like a standard business model? We all know when we go into restaurants the cost is the one thing you never see coming. Four dollars for a sirloin and lobster with four pounds of shrimp on the side is always nice but where biscuits and gravy cost four thousand dollars it kind of hurts. I mean it is kind of outrageous that biscuits and gravy is going to cost me four thousand dollars. It seems that the guy next to me getting to have biscuits and gravy for two hundred dollars is a little unfair until the waiter points out that I did enjoy them, so I see he didn't have to pay the enjoyment fee of three thousand eight hundred dollars. I can't complain too much since he did choke and die right there. I'm sure they will track down his wife to pay the balance, you know, after they add on the fact that he died to the bill.

High Rants

You shouldn't inconvenience someone just because you died on their watch, that is just cruel. Here in Oklahoma, we are having American citizens that are dying in earthquakes. What kind of hatred for America can you have when you so carelessly die due to oil companies desire to make profits, no matter what else it costs? How can we burden a company with dying due to their refusal to be regulated and make safe products? When a failure of regulation has taken trillions from the American economy with the great recession by itself not to mention the thousands of company that turned land worthless around the country due to disasters that they could easily be see coming. Making them prove that deregulation isn't going to harm the economy or anything else is just to high of a burden to place on them. With a constant talk of how regulations are bad for companies how could we be so cruel to hold them to not harming us and use the fact that deregulation has killed more jobs than anything else against them. So just plan your deaths ahead of time, okay?

The funeral business will appreciate it. You can't be dumped into the ground however you see fit with nothing lost in translation. Just plan your funeral and jump into the ovens, if you are a pussy you can shoot yourself after you climb in. I can guarantee you that a real man would just let the cremation process take it's natural course. We know that getting cremated does the job nicely so there is no need to pretend you are doing it for any other reason than you don't want to be roasted alive. If you are being so fussy about how your body is prepared before they toss it into the oven might I suggest some basil, thyme, salt, pepper and a lemon bath beforehand. Periodic basting through the cooking process will ensure that your skin will be nice and crispy when you are done.

When you spend the last part of your paycheck just to see the woman you love smile. Just five on a package of smoke is all it takes, even though she taste like an ashtray afterwards you don't mind. She is just a pretty little thing. New love when there is absolutely no jaded shell left. Turning the winter days to a gently embracing spring as summer days are coming you can even hear the birds singing. No telling what she will turn into after you get caught, spending the night with her sister. What you need to know is never get caught spending the night with your wives' sister. Never forget that feeling when the woman that you love smiles because when she spins out that is the only thing you can hold onto.

Later on it is so easy to forget as things get in the way and your conversations turn boring. Sink into that memory of what you had and try to find it again. Otherwise, I would suggest starting at the beginning with someone new unless you are old or ugly because it is likely that you will be just giving up the last person that will ever love you. I mean really stand at the mirror and look at yourself and if you cannot answer yes to the question. Would I do me? Then you need to reconsider that nice person that puts up with your ass and lets you have sex with them. If you want to complain about not enough sex might I suggest you get off your ass and do something nice for her. A back rub for no reason once a week or telling her she is beautiful can go a long way to getting those bulky sweets off when you get into bed.

We need to accept that relationships are just a contract where you are constantly renegotiating what kind of life your willing to put up with. You can break pieces of the contract sometimes but all the time will end your access to them. If everyone went through the effort of verbalizing what they want you might not end up together but you might still be able to get into their bed. I have the last five ex-girlfriends still in my life. What I mean is, how many times have you heard "*let's stay friends*" and it happened? My exs just won't go away and I still get to play. Do you hear that, if you just tell the truth the entire time you can still get access to them long after you shouldn't be able to. Like if one of them got married to a fat fuck that can't see his dick, I shouldn't be able to still stick it in there. There is one thing that you might know but have never put it into words and I would like to help you out. Never have sex with a married woman… whose husband has had a vasectomy. How many kids can you blame on his vasectomies not taking? I would really like to know because with each kid it seems to be getting harder.

Whenever you have a girl pregnant it isn't the worst thing to check. I mean you know they are attractive enough to have sex so you shouldn't doubt that they would be able to get another man. So just making sure is being respectful to her and her competence. Personally I use, I got a vasectomy so this kid can't be mine. Now you might be a little upset but what is worse the fact that none of the girls that I used it on are sure that it was my kid or that I have lied about a vasectomy? There are worse things to do than just watch as a bus runs someone over. You might have never seen it before so it could constitute that you are living life to the fullest. That does fulfill part of the meaning of life. You could scream out so he sees the bus. That would be good but you could also scream out, "*Say hi to God for me.*" I would put that as worse than keeping your mouth shut. So I might not be the best in the world but clearly I can be so much worse than I currently am. I think the worst would be to flip him off and swear so his last moments are as bad as they could be.

High Rant 4 Extra Verification

    I'll have to start you somewhere else than the beginning. Not for any aesthetics I assure you, I just started this when I was outside smoking because I'm not a total asshole. I am speaking to you, the complete asshole that smokes inside where everyone has to sleep.

    Coming to this point has taken awhile now. When you get to the point of being a God things kind of change. I mean in a million years, humans will be for all purposes essentially immortal. Where you can only die if you set forth to wipe yourself out of existence. First, you would have to enter your password because this is serious shit, that is about to go down. I'm going to also want to see a verification email. It wouldn't be *"Well, I'm done with this shit"* comment and the computer keeping you alive shuts off.

    Then things will naturally go off over the deep end because of the just one more ID verification step and you'll be done with the world. That would just send me over the edge. And when you finally get to the fuck it just delete everything menu they naturally will give you more options. Would you like to put your life to sleep for two week to infinity? Maybe you would just like to enter the ghost mode? You know, you could be sliding unobserved though the life's of all those that you have known. It could take eons to go through all the options. How about a basic reset we start you off in heaven like it's your first day again it seems like it is one of your personal favorites, you've selected deleting your memory a few thousand times already. Doesn't that seem like the decision that you are going to make? We'll just need a secondary email verification for that selection. Is it the same email address question that brings you to "WHAT DO YOU MEAN I NEED ANOTHER EMAIL VERIFICATION, THIS IS HEAVEN ARE YOU INSANE?"

    That is a popular response this year but your email it is still 45B45DAE45@heaven right. Okay, now the verification email should arrive in your inbox in the next thirty to forty years. Don't hit resend or the reset or it will resend and then we will have to wait for the second email because that one will be considered the requested email while the first one will be null and voided. If we get the unrequested email that means you will have to talk to my manager. At this point you are wondering what other options are they going to give you before it is all over with.

High Rant 5 Terminal IQ velocity

You know, I don't blame Clinton looking at an intern inquiring that she get him two hands and a face so he can finish his clock as he dropped his pants. That isn't his fault. We know, we would have done the same in that situation, have you seen her spread in the nudie magnetize. It's the presidency; the quickest way to raise your success rate with the ladies.

Just walk up to any girl in the place, look her up and down like it's your job. (Captain Kirk's Voice kicks in, Just back...there...and here.) Speaking those words, those, special words "I am, protecting your freedom, to go home, with, whoever, you wish. I, should, get a reward. Where are, we, going?"

There is dignity in doing that, what else could be done. The thing that I blame him for, is not just admitting it. It wasn't anything different that every other politician. They will never just say yes, even though we know it and they know it true and they know that we know it. Still refuse to admit that he let one out, took the bribe, slept with a stripper or what his policy on the strengthening of the dollar against the depressed China's currency. We get the same thing every time and that bothers me. The problem was the scale of it. She was hot, beyond belief that she had any kind of brains in her head. You mean to tell me, the brain dead hottie that hangs around the president hasn't been doing her constitutional duties. I mean the scale of it. It was like we just watched someone on live television stab a knife into a guy a dozen times when you scream what have you done. He replies "depends what you mean by done but at this time I'm going to place my faith in god these days. There isn't any problem that he can't fix as long as we let the spirit of this nation free."

It's amazing how much that sounded like an old chief at a powwow praising to the heathen gods. Maybe it was a bad idea to put the capital building over an Indian graveyard? Well the land was cheap? Cost them a lot though.

With Clinton's denials derailments distraction answers just (made my head twist up and to the left Denials Derailments Distraction ANSWERS did it again) reminded me of the worst kid in the world. You would always know he did it but he refuses to say it was him. Like if he lied on top of what he did he'll get away with it. I was sitting there watching him mess everything up and he refuse to even acknowledge that he was currently doing it. THE REASON because he's been getting away with IT... How is this not so astonishing easy to understand. You're not punishing him or it's not enough. If you don't punish him for anything he does he'll do whatever he wants. If you make him sit in the corner for five minutes because he was caught stealing a cop car, it isn't going to work. This point you can see that he isn't the one to be blamed.

You can train a dog sit, stay, roll over and such. They are fairly easy to train in just about anything you want. Birds, horses, rodents even the house cat. They have trained flat worms to never take a left turn. I mean these flat worms are incapable of taking a left turn, physically incapable due to proper training. If certain death was to their right and sex and food is to their left. They would swim right in to the jaws of a waiting fish. So what make you think that you can't train a kid not to fuck up. What makes them so different than a FUCKING DOG? I mean seriously is it their bigger brain that makes it impossible to not leave their things all over the house. If because they are smarter than dog they need to make mistakes then, I would love to travel to the future so I can see the terminal velocity of IQ. If being smarter makes you break the rules there is a point as we get smarter that we just can't obey a single rule. Don't stab your friend with that butcher knife. Use English if you want to get something. JFffff   laaa fuJ   ? Makes perfect sense.

Since we are talking about going through time as something that could be fun. Looking back, today we marvel at those that were the pinnacle of cool. We look at James Dean and say he was fucking awesome. How could it possibly be that someone that cool ever existed surrounding by his contemporaries? The Fonz, they thought that he was cool; we don't even have to look at the jumping sharks on ski while wearing a leather jacket incident. Douche. Look at all the famous people at that time, the women are fine and the men.... Women had it hard back in the day. With all the Back in My Day That Was Cool talk we have to put up with.

I mean women's lives must have been hard. With all the assaulting, sexual harassment and rape going on that they had to put up with, men that are so uncool that today the only ones on their Facebook friends list would be their mom and grandma. Not even the fathers would be able to acknowledge that they were there kids without dying of embarrassment. How bad does it have to get to where you father would rather say that he can't keep his wife happy insinuating that she might be sleeping with the entire town just to put the doubt in everyone's mind that you might not be his. Add on top of that we have people so incredibly average when it comes to their bedroom skills that women didn't even get to have a little freak session. Not even a single day of being tied to a bed as mental patient as you perform an exorcism. Or even just putting her over your knee and saying "Who's your Daddy?" Getting in on Incest Role Playing? Yeah, that is what you are doing. You, my sick friend need to pay attention to what you say.

The English language is a sacred gift passed down to us from the great civilization of western culture. Yeah, does sound weird, doesn't it? With the complete co-opting of Western Civilization for the propaganda of the KKK and Nazis we wake up now to the incredibly hard reality when we say that we are awesome. We are the safest we have ever been in all of human history. The lowest crime we ever had and not only that, we are still adding crimes, beating and raping your wife wasn't fully outlawed till the mid 1990s. Women had a truly hard time. But that doesn't matter if you don't work together. Western Culture dominates this world because we cherry picked the best parts of our past and every other culture.

Cherry picking the best parts of our past does lead to some problems but it also has given us the best tool for domination on this planet. Free markets, regulated to protect the public. Anti corruption and competition for the benefit of society and a thousand other benefits has given us control of the world. Where our culture has produced tremendous gains other cultures mimicked. Where they make money or profit we will surly culturally appropriate it. Why is that any different from China using capitalism to move out of third would stats? Culture appropriation has been how every culture around the world has worked. If we didn't we would have thousands of independent cultures with their own unique languages, buildings, gods. Where every family would have to invent new tools as those that invented the old ones have died out. Yeah, that world falls apart real quickly.

So the English language should be respected and you should watch what you say. If we diminish the English language you would no longer be able to understand what I just said. Which we can all agree that would be a bad thing. With hundreds of years we can still look back and read the poetry and epic tales of our past. Gaining a brief glimpse of what it was back then, because that is all that you want. Time travel into the past, is like trying to pound your dick flat with a ball-peen hammer. It's a bad idea. The past where you get to be burned as a witch, right. That past. Or are we talking about the middle ages where you need royal blood or you can be killed, enslaved, raped, maimed or anything else nobility wanted to do with you.

The idealization of the past comes from the cherry picking. We forget the plagues that wiped out a third of the population while they weren't concerned that it was the end of the world because that shit happened all the time. With disease, child birth, the raids, war and just noble killing the surfs for fun the chance you're going to die early is quite large. It would be more thrilling but so would playing Russian roulette. Yes life is more boring now but think of all the good things, like fake tits. They only had those for a couple decades now. Plus the bras are so much better than they used to be. Tits are up and out, western culture is awesome. There is something to be said for butts, but you can't look at them when you are talking to girls. It just doesn't work that way. If you want to see butts just let them catch you watching their chest.

That is among women's other most irritating traits that modern man has to put up with. I mean why can't women just sleep with the desperate men. Modern society is so incredibly dangerous because women can't control the most pathetic men. Going without for so long you become a loser and no one will ever look up to you again. Seeing terrorist attacks you look at the guys and say "Ya, that guy is a complete loser. He probably never got any?" Yes if you attack innocent people just because you can't get your dick sucked, it's sad. Come on, does anyone here think that these terrorist aren't pathetic? Exactly. We all know how pathetic these guys are we just have to admit it, vocally. I mean more people die in the United States by falling out of bed than in all the terrorist attacks each year. Yes, you heard that right. People falling out of bed kills more people in the United States every year than all the terrorist groups Al-Qaida, Boko Haram, KKK or even Shrinners.

You know what else kills a lot of people every year in the United States. Tragic masturbation accidents. Yes, I'm talking about unintended deaths due to having a great organism. We should all look on those that die every year as the tragedy it is. Do you think someone dying isn't a tragedy? See. Over two hundred people in the United States die from this each year. I'm starting a charity to bring to light this endemic problem we are facing in this society that has a higher death toll than Americans killed in terrorist events in the United States.

I'm calling on every American to see what we have here. The needless deaths of people just for liking a superior orgasm. With your donation we can work to stop the tragic deaths of more people than died in terrorist attacks in the US over the last thirty years. Six trillion to get revenge at the death of three thousand people. Doesn't feel good, does it? What is worse taking the six trillion that we used to get revenge that could have saved millions if we used it on more productive pursuits.

High Rant 6 Immortality Science

When looking at philosophical thought that we had throughout the ages we can only conclude a single undeniable fact. There is a massive detour in the 60s to almost childlike stupidity. I mean at a level of modern philosophical thought the large minds of the 60s are about as rigorous as Aristotle or Plato. I mean, come on the things that we are really talking about, are so far advanced it's like the difference where philosophical thought is and where the general public assumes it is. I mean it isn't like we could let the public know where the philosophical thought is, that would make all the little jokes about people not understanding useless because laughing at them from behind their backs is the whole purpose.

That is something that we couldn't possibly allow. We must be allowed to continue to make fun of the general public for the reason that could be none other than we just want to feel superior to you. I mean it isn't like we would do anything to be able to convey that global warming is a real thing and we are going to suffer tremendously if we don't do anything about it. Where all we do is spend billions to find the truth in the universe just to hide facts from the general public so we can feel good about ourselves. I mean it isn't just easy enough to point to the fact that ninety nine percent of the economy is due to scientific research. Science is the reason that you live a long, healthy life. Breast implants yeah that is science, bitches. I mean it couldn't be easy for politicians to get the fuck out of the way. See, so since it isn't that easy the next logical conclusion that we can come to is we are trying to not explain ourselves properly.

I do have hope for humanity but to believe scientists are trying to explain things so no one can understand what is being said is just insane. I'm sorry there seems to be a problem with your science as it doesn't add up. Science isn't as profitable if you are wrong or even a little off. Of course we get it a little off just so we can cut down the science budgets that we get. I mean it is sensible, if science didn't work as awesome as it does now, you could set it aside but it is so incredibly perfect when you are looking for the best way to get a return on the money that the government spends. Need to improve your economy, spend on science. Need to live longer, spend on science. Need to fuck your third trophy wife since you are rich and can do whatever you want, spend on science because not only will we give you that little blue pill but we will be those that might make you immortal, just so you can take trophy wife hunting to a professional level for those that just doesn't have the kind of money that you have can be amazed at how life can be once you're rich.

High Rants

If you are looking for any type of life you want and have the money to pay for it, it is science that you want. Spend it now and before you die you might just have the chance to become the first immortal. For how could changing the very nature of humanity a creature that grows learns and then passes on for a new generation to come forward carrying the torch of humanity into the future. Into a creature that lives eternally without a second thought of having children to pass on to the next generation of his family the wealth that he acquired in his short time here. I'm sure that living forever wouldn't unalterable change your chances for the hereafter. Opinions can be changed we know all it take is some cash. Now for all those that aren't rich enough to afford the immortality serum will instead get a yearly payment. Because, believing that living forever is a morally justifiable position and those that decide to live forever shouldn't be judged for choosing a morally superior life than those that can't afford it. Those that live forever should be judged on their best 100 year stretch when they were alive so they aren't punished for living life to its fullest.

Now as everyone that dies has to take the mandatory payment for the next year every human believes that those upper class shouldn't be punished for living a more morally superior life than we do. Now those that say that this is a system that benefits the rich how dare you complain after you took the mandatory money. As anyone beyond this earth complains about letting the rich off completely without any moral responsibility we got to point out that our race has different kinds of values than you and you should be respectful of different belief systems, unless we could completely wipe out an inferior alien race from the universe. It is like we were totally justified in doing it. Always take the side of humanity those aliens aren't like us and no one is going to be missing them anyways.

Now as the scientific community is the ones that are important due to ensuring that the immortality serum still works and making hard-ons harder you would like us around and working on solving the problems of the universe. Like how we can become an even stronger power for those pesky aliens that don't think you deserve to treat us like that. Now, does that clear up what we want to do as scientist. We want to answer the questions of the universe and if you don't understand that then you are dumb.

I mean how stupid can someone be and still be a functional person. For hundreds of years all science has been is a dick measuring contest saying ha that nice but check this out. Ba bam. Yeah, It's large and you should see the statistics that back this baby up. After all that time you expect us not to point out where someone fucked up. I mean the anti-science groups acts like a tranny walks into a high school locker room and everyone pretends nothing is happening.

She/he is like everyone else and when you are teenagers without a complete understand of your own sexuality would easily relate in a productive way to someone that is clearly an outsider in your community and should be made to feel welcome in this clearly precious place where every deformity that someone might expose as they have to strip down to get into Gym Gear should just be ignored. Why would we use something like that to attack Sir Jiggles or Lady Downthere? There is just so much childishness in the world. We just have to not lash out due to our insecurity.

Insecurity is a problem when you are taking on high risk living, like becoming immortal. As such the scientific community has developed a program that will decrease insecurity for any problem that you are facing in living forever. This program also comes in surrogate mode where we take the course for you and tell you how well you did. If you don't feel comfortable having someone doing things for you might we suggest you take "I'm rich I deserve it" it is a great course to take as your position in this world, it is cruel for you not to put those lowly dregs to work. How else will they know they should feel bad for how horrible they are to you. Now if the surrogate mode isn't to your liking do to the decreased effectiveness that the surrogate mode offers it also comes in medication. Mild side effects but must be included in your daily medication for your desired reality. If you want to completely remove insecurity than we might suggest brain surgery. You'll never have insecurity ever again. Side effects are flawless bravery you might try to stop an engine with your bare hands. You'll pick up women no matter how inappropriate it is that you are doing it. Great for those professional trophy wife athletes. New things have their own drawbacks from seeing a moon of the desert in winter, to being involved sexually with all that crossing your path.

We offer solutions to every problem that the world faces or that you are willing to pay me for answering your one stop shop in getting exactly what you want. I will not point out that this is clearly how super villains get started. It couldn't be the ability to produce anything that you want in your home garage with 3D printers and a few grad students that starts super villain layers. There had to be some other thing that causes people to act insane. The whole super villain thing sounds great, yeah, I'm serious, great idea. What about if you win, you get to spend the rest of your life looking over your shoulder for someone stabbing a knife into your back. If you rule the world you will be the single person standing in the way of every other person doing anything. Understand that. If you rule it all, everyone will want to kill you before they do anything. Even if it is a shit. "Ahh! God, I have to go to the bathroom. Wow, look the evil overlord." Boom he dead. I'm not sure how this isn't understood.

The kidnappings is great fun, I mean if you want to try to make any sort of contribution to humanity you just got to get used to the monthly kidnapping by rich trust fund kids that were happy to take over. With secret layers that have been build behind every dry cleaners, dungeon abandoned by trolls during their most philosophical periods. With towering constructions that can't be distinguished from caves. It was the trolls most expansive contribution to society ironically they lived like they did years earlier. Yes, trust fund kids that have their evil hideout in fucking caves just refuses to play along with others. So if you would like to do anything for the benefit of society you must either spend half of the year being a kidnap victim or go to work for one of the heroic wealthy people that is going to combat this scourge on our citizens. Help them build up power outside of the law, building their base to state of the art perfection with the help of their endless money supply. So that they effortlessly win for the benefit of our country. Soon you will be going toe to toe with some of the worst people on the face of this earth. They have spent their fortunes to subvert the will of the human race and now you stand in their way having someone that will block anyone that thinks he can inflict his will on everyone. Locked in an endless battle to prevent them from taking over the world. Your only hope is you'll soon get to see the end of this battle as the forces of darkness are pushed out of the world. We know that this is the truth because we will machine gun down anyone that stands in our way, for we are the good guys.

Spend money on science because if it isn't possible at least we will do everything that we can to get you as close to it. You'll know that it is truth because that is what we do and at the very least we'll stick you in a recliner, give you some VR goggles and psychedelics.

High Rant 7 Fuckface

When looking at what you're going to be doing with your life you must decide how much effort your willing to put into it. As I described in my book "The Meaning of Life and Other Useless Crap" which obviously you read. I mean you had to read a serious pamphlet on the most important philosophical question of all time before you read this mind intoxicating bitching. I mean, with the world as is what can you do that is better than reading me to sooth the pain? I get it, the world can be a hard and an unforgiving place but since you know the meaning of life you can easily understand. Where you have the feeling that you don't want to put effort into the world but feeling you must. Then you think about Fuckface and no matter how much effort it would take to get it, it still would be worth it.

Let me tell you about Fuckface. He is a man/woman/doesn't matter who always upsets those around him. I mean everybody knows Fuckface. You know Fuckface he's always screwing up something. Remember the time Fuckface drove your dad's car into the police station? Or how about when he got your sister pregnant or your mom? I mean that Fuckface. What won't he get up on? There literally no telling. I'm an author and I'm literally using that word correctly.

Putting in the work to be a famous artist just so I can paint a permanent instillation in a gallery. I would go in when there is when no one around. Pull out my stencil to add a new piece of art to the museum. They would all come in and be like where is it? I got to see it. Finding it in some obscure corner only a few inches high. Getting down onto their knees to see it. Crawling over to it. Squinting hard to get it in view. Recognizing who it is and freaking the fuck out. GOD DAM IT! IT'S FUCKFACE. Yes, go back over that last sentence, it is Fuckface. I mean doesn't that entire paragraph change for everyone, it is instead Fuckface. Goes from one of excitement to one of a perverted mess.

But that is the miracle of Fuckface isn't it. No matter what happens you can count on Fuckface to mess it all up. Forever in our lives, just to screw it up. So doesn't it stand that he should be memorialized in art. Nothing else in our culture is so important but has never become art. No one wants to make art of Fuckface. But putting a portrait of Fuckface in a museum where he'll remain until the end of time. Yeah, you didn't realize that if I get to install a permanent art work in a museum we get to stick Fuckface where no one in the world but him could fuck up your life. I mean if we could find a place to put Fuckface where he couldn't screw up your life, he wouldn't be Fuckface anymore now would he?

High Rants

Getting Fuckface would be and admiral accomplishment of your life. I mean seriously. Getting to be a great artist that a museum would allow him to be added to their permanent collection of art sight unseen. They would trust the artist so much that he gets unrestricted access to a museum. How wouldn't that be a great accomplishment? I mean becoming one of the greatest artist of your era doesn't that fulfill the meaning of life?

I hate to be meta here but since I'm the one that answered the meaning of life question, does that mean I fulfilled it? Who would have thought that there would be questions after the meaning of life was solved? Philosophy teachers and students. There is always more questions. I have answered a question no one could answer for tens of thousands of years does it mean I fulfilled my purpose? I could go beyond just giving humanity the answers to the meaning of existence but it doesn't seem like it would make much difference. I could save thousands of people and you would say about me is I solved the meaning to the existence of all humanity and he saved thousands of orphans from a meteor that one time by single handedly catching it. Like throwing half an hour onto eternity. Doesn't everything seem like it will only be a pittance now? Fifty extra dollars when you have a billion. Winning lifetime achievement award for your impressive work at your kindergarten graduation.

High Rant 8 Universes

I don't know how Ryan Reynolds did it. I mean you think about what happened the first time that he played Deadpool. There does seem to be some reason that they kept trying him. How about Green Lantern remember that blockbuster. How about the role he played in Blade 3 and that franchise never made another movie. Dogs with split lower jaws? Was that his idea? How about his TV show Zeroman that was a disaster or was it? I'm not sure, was it worth spending my time? I'm sorry, how many seasons did it have, yeah one. Anytime that he got anywhere near a superhero franchise it become a flop either it is because of a curse or we just can't take him seriously when he is the one saving the day.

I went to see Deadpool and it was amazing. How could it come from, this guy? Four time loser makes good. There is almost a movie in just that. He couldn't succeed just a born loser, there was no help for him but a world full of people that kept giving him chances again and again and again. Even though everyone knows that he didn't earned it. In a world that doesn't even let the born losers fail one finally does something cool. Come see the monkey that typed Shakespeare. With that said what would have happened if Wonder Woman flopped?

In a world where we have three Hulk movies, three reboots of the Spiderman franchise, and Ryan Reynolds playing two iterations of Deadpool how is it that everyone reading this knows that everyone else reading this is thinking the same thing. Where can I sign up for a boat to Themyscira? It is a great movie but it still isn't something that is transformative, except in the aspect that we had the greatest DC Universe movie since Batman Begins. There is hope that DC can make it big on the silver screen again. Yeah a female lead and director, about and women that was created by a man written by a man for decades and was drawn by men. If we have to celebrate every step along the way there will be no room left for advancement. It's like arguing what universe you want to go into.

When contemplating leaving this Universe you got to answer this. Are you willing to give up on the impact that you will make in this Universe? Then you remember the reason that you want to go into a make believe Universe is because the life you have here will do nothing for the future of humanity and your impact on the universe will be nothing. So you're up to living in another Universe and what you got to remember it is you that is going into another Universe, not Superman. You only get the skills that you have now. How pathetic are you? Now that the rules are not in question we should continue.

High Rants

If you enter a world where humans can use magic you can as well. If it is the Harry Potter's Universe you will be a muggle. You only get magic if everyone in your Universe can use it since they live there, you have to pass the requirements for any ability.

Travel into another Universe is permanent and happens all at once. There is no sending things to you on a pre-worked out schedule. You only get what you take.

Once you enter your Universe you will put ripples as the Universe starts to change so everything that happens after you get there is a logical progression of the world. You don't get to kill someone and have their objects just float around so nothing is changed in the world.

With the less the obvious rules in place we can start to decide where we would like to go on our exile from reality. Personally I would go to the Universe of "Is It Wrong to Pick Up Girls In a Dungeon" it's a nice middle area between the middle age fantasy that we have when looking back and not remembering that it was a cesspool of illness and death when fantasizing about Camelot. There is a dungeon filled with monsters that you can slaughter on an endless loop of kill, get money for the kills, party, blow all your money, wake up and kill again. There is absolutely nothing that is morally objectionable since the dungeon was built by the gods for their entertainment and gives humans a place to vent their violent urges. Like the purge but not stupid. So any killing you're doing in the dungeon is what the gods want, thus slaughtering monsters is fulfilling the desire of the gods so it is automatically the moral thing to do. I have never been waste deep in blood saying "Man, I'm such a righteous servant of the lord" I guess that I could do it in our universe but I think that some people might having a problem with that and object to my characterization of my actions.

So when you are thinking about what Universe to take, you got to know that you are not picking a better Universe than the one you are living in. You are selecting a place that is fun and entertaining until you die. Just like in this universe your impact will be about what you have now. When looking at fictitious Universes you have to see that they are created by a writer that wanted a place for something shitty to happened. We aren't creating a universe that destiny will be molding a continuing advancement of society with just enough strife to teach people to be kinder every generations with humanity reaching for enlightenment of all the intelligent creatures in creation. Our Universe's are broken, so we can fuck with those that live in them. Yes, you will be going into a Universe that was only created to mess with the lives of the people that you will be spending the rest of your life with.

There are some Universes that no one would choose. Like The Man in the High Castle that is a horrible world not even Nazi's of today would want to go to that one. Yeah, I know they act all big and bad and you given them the option to go join others and they go all yellow. Probably has something to do with all the DNA test coming back and saying that they aren't part of the pure white race after all. I don't know what their problem would be other than the immediate execution that they would be facing. Hilarious, no papers.

So with some of the pitfalls out of the way we can look at what we would like DC or Marvel. I mean there are some others but when we start breaking them in it comes down to DC or Marvel. They are the ones that are paying me for saying that so they clearly won a systematic impartial analysis into what universes you get to pick from.

High Rant 9 Legally Binding Contract

I know, one day I'll be in the White House wondering why I did it. I mean I'm not a zealot or a megalomaniac why would I ever want this? I should just sit back and complain that someone else hasn't done what I wanted them to do. That would have been the simple solution. But, nooo. I had to go all "Sure there are many paths that I can take to the presidency" and it was challenge accepted. So after that part of my life nothing that came after can be construed to be my fault.

Yes, that is what we are doing here. We are deciding in advance that nothing I do as the President of the United States can possible be my fault. I mean whatever I get us into I cannot be held as the responsible party because this right here makes a legally binding contract with all Americans. Any kind of loss of limb wouldn't be my fault. Or, say someone's childhood home had to be targeted by a drone strike. I will assuredly not be doing that because I deleted him from the High School yearbook and he thinks he has the nerve to upset me by thinking fondly about his childhood home. That shit just won't fly.

Or if someone's entire life and existence was deleted. I'm sure there isn't a press delete button. It's obvious, Ted Cruz would have already been deleted even Obama couldn't resist that. Cruz does look like someone tried to delete him, kind of like a three week old corpse wax sculpture that was left in the sun to long. It's one of those would you go back and kill Hitler questions. The answer is always yes. Even if you are going back in pink panties and have to do it with a large black dildo. The answer is yes, in polite company. I don't make the rules, I just ensure that they are stuck to making sure everyone knows their place. So if someone hasn't shaven their legs so they are baby smooth on a first date it is very clear that she should die alone. Someone that disgusting must be crazy and not willing to put in the work to land herself a man. Maybe she can toss herself at a married man old enough to be her father.

I'll let you in on a secret study that I have taken on the research in the past few months. I've been laying the ground work into the philosophical study of the philosophy of the sixty's. How and where they went wrong. Could the weed of the sixties brought them down all the wrong paths? Or was it their stupidity? I have been taking large dosages and still can't get high enough to think the hippy way. As a dedicated researcher I'm going to keep at it and find out does long term effects of exposure provide any conversion over time. When I'm finished with this study I'll expect to be sending the latest New York Times bestselling novel about my exploits of rock star, astronaut, secret agent, scientist, gods life in October. With the definitive work on the stupidity of the sixties philosophy in book stores for your holiday Christmas shopping. I'll be expecting to be knocking down four Nobels this year. I don't know if I'll get the fifth. That peace award isn't completely in the bag all I did was completely eliminated the threat of nuclear weapons.

It was a simple thing I sure someone else would have figured it out eventually. All you had to do was tie the elimination of nuclear weapons to various geopolitical arrangements that provides a massive benefit while removing all damage or potential losses to the participating nations while continuing to increase the cost on the nations that refuses to give them up. It was so simple I'm sure you all totally knew that already plus I assured them that they all have a perfectly adequate penis size and they should be very proud of it. If I get it, I get it but you know you win one of these there all just happy to know you but six in a row seems a little over indulgent.

The real winners of my awards…is the people that help me. I'm throwing this out to all of you. Ether you followed me, friended me, retweeted me, or hollered at me these Nobel trophies are because of you. I mean everyone of you that has threatened to murder the Nobel committee or burn down colleges, towns or even entire nations have won them. It was all for me. I know that you have been putting in the work to let everyone know that they are not allowed to win. While our colleges around the world are putting in their second best effort in all areas. You can't fault them for that. Who wants their kids dragged through the streets after stopping me from getting another Nobel Prize.

I have to give you all the credit that your work deserves. You would not believe how easy it is to negotiate peace when one word from me and everyone the guy loves will die within fifteen minutes. Man you should see their faces when I threaten to kill everyone in their family that had their shoelaces tied on the inside that day. Negotiating makes so much more sense to them than just having everyone they loved killed. You get to see them beg first. "See, much better to negotiate with me rather than get your entire family killed."

If you don't want to kill them but you want them gone there has only been one way that has ever worked. All the plans to exterminate a people in the past has failed. Think of it, of all the groups that have been targeted in the past there are all still here Jews, Chinese, Native Americas, mimes, I mean no matter how we try, you just can't kill enough. There has been one way and it is the only way. We fuck them to death. Wait hold on. Sorry, I literally mean we fuck them out of existence. We did it to the cave men and they are no longer here, right? I mean we came into Europe and seen this hunched over thick browed creature with a hair body living in caves and it was like yup, sign me up for that kink. Over the next few hundred years we hunted them all, then fucked them out of existence. I mean do you see any cave men around here? No, No you do not.

Since that is only way we are going to get rid of anyone. I mean it's not like we could get rid of the Mimes. No one will fuck a Mime. Get it. Their creepy and clearly there is something very wrong with their souls. So there is only one thing, Cassidy how about we go out and have some fun? I'm a solution finder clearly we should get together. If it is the religious differences you only eat bacon through a hole that you cut in a sheet. I've fucked your sister. In my defense we hadn't started dating yet so she still kind of has first dibs, but, I was sure to get her permission to what is totally going to happen between us. Just so you know that we are going to click, I have a thing for sisters.

That does have other implications. Now that we know for a fact that we can fuck a species out of existence and have already done it. Is that the reason we haven't been visited? I do understand that the rednecks are preparing for wide spread raping of aliens when they land. Would that alone keep the aliens away? I wouldn't be so scared of that possibility if it wasn't for the fact that I've been to the upper floors at the alien conventions. We are talking about nerds working together for the last few decades. Do you really think they weren't up to something? I'm talking robotic alien sex machines. They ship them in, in pieces and put them together in the high end suites. I'll tell you what, they make the little Anime sex robots look like a pinto. I'm serious, anything less looks like last year's model and that is something you wouldn't let anyone see you in.

I have my little sex robot shame in the closet. I can't even look at it. I have to turn off the lights before I open the door. I got one of the glow n the dark chassis so you know exactly where to stick it, just to be safe. I'm looking into getting my own reptilian sex slave doll. Top of the line comes with the conversion adjustments so it can grow male reproductive organs as well.

Now the quest is how far can I push talk of Sex Robots until you skip to the next chapter. You ever go on a date and look at the girl and think 'Yeah, this isn't going to be working out.' At that point in time do you think to yourself I'm a good person so dropping them like a rock would be mean? However, you are also a dick and think 'I wonder how far I can go before she runs screaming from this restaurant?' And now we reach the philosophy point about blame from where I started. I have indicated that if you go on a date with me and bore me, I'll proceed to treat you worse by the minute until I break you just for the fun of it. I can now safely do this to any woman that I date and be cleared ethically for my actions because this is clearly a legally binding contract.

High Rant 10 Enough to Get You Killed

    I think, that I have made it clear my feelings when it comes to people having extraordinary gifts and just wasting them playing superhero. So with that, what powers would you get? Something obvious like Superman's setup where all you get to do is be a glorified firefighter. It's not a bad thing, I guess, in the off hours you can do the work of thousands of construction workers. Yeah, you. I sure the thousands of construction workers that are sitting on their ass instead of working will change the world.

    With the entire set of thing before us it isn't really that many you get to choose from. Magneto if you would be willing to work as a construction worker you'll make billions every year. Xavier is great, you get to turn the most powerful people in the world into your dolls and that is about it. There are others like god mode, every game has a god mode, but how long will it be until you get bored with it.

    Isn't that the trick. Just don't get bored with life. Have it just difficult enough to get you involved but not enough to get you killed.

High Rant 11 Erotic Asphyxiation

    Modern American society is the best of all others. When it is more likely to die in a tragic masturbation accident than from terrorism, why are you scared? But we spent 5 trillion to go after a few dirt dwellers and nothing to stem the tide of clogged arteries. With hundreds of thousands dying from Big Mac every year we could have had 5 trillion spent on getting people healthy. Free food for every American and everyone around the world as long as it is healthy. That would have eliminated millions dying. Every year going back fifty years, less than sixty die on American soil from terrorism while over two hundred die from erotic asphyxiation.
    I'll offering my services, any beautiful woman that likes erotic asphyxiation is welcome in my bed for the safety of your heart's desires.

High Rant 12 Hamburger

I don't have any reference for what happened. It seems like there isn't anything in the history of mankind that brings us to an understanding on this point. A critical mass of conspiracy theories that spit forth an entire political party completely removed from the most basic rewards of a democracy. We have an entire political party that doesn't have the right to vote. How can that happen in one of the most powerful countries in the world?

It seems strange to put it this way but when we see that nothing that a republican runs on has any basis in reality we end up with only one conclusion. Republicans can't make an informed vote and only an informed vote makes it a democracy and allows you to say you have the right to vote. If I were to give you the vote between getting ice cream and a whooping you'd choose the ice cream. The problem with this is with the ice cream you get higher crime, lower wages, poorly educated children, more pregnant teens, less rights, a whooping and you don't get to eat the ice cream. I mean why would you get to eat the ice cream without the regulations it was just arsenic and food coloring in the first place. In all seriousness elections where you get to vote for anything that you want doesn't matter if everything that you see gets filtered so you aren't voting for what you want.

You can easily imagine an entire group of people that don't believe anything they see because they have been conditioned their entire life. This isn't the source of your problem, you are obviously under attack by someone outside of your community and if given a fair chance you wouldn't be the pathetic loser that you are. Hearing things like that for years could make you start to believe that you are capable of more than you are. Pathetic losers will and forever be pathetic losers. There is no need to pretend that they are capable because we can see where pathetic losers might get it into their heads that they could run a country.

Where the media is ignoring that they require hundreds of billions a year to subsidize red states so they don't get upset that we are talking about their short comings. After all we are good enough neighbors to hand them hundreds of billions each year shouldn't we also be kind enough not to rub their noise in it. I mean we have only been doing this for a few decades soon their magical economic policies will start taking effect. Any day now and we'll be sorry that we ever teased them for being racist bigots we just didn't know that they were waiting for the policies to kick in providing republicans with massive increases in wealth pulling them out of poverty, instantly removing all the extra crime, making their kids healthier and smarter. I speak for everyone none of us would have guessed that it would just take thirty years with no evidence of it working before it did and being better educated it is easy to see how we wouldn't be able to see the where the profit is once again and take it for ourselves. It isn't like we have been doing that for decades already.

Consent is needed for those to be ruled; information is needed to chose. It is all well and good for a game show but if you needed to make all your decisions by choosing one or two. "Dam, I thought that I was going to get a hamburger." That scenario makes what you are choosing a game where you assume you don't know the outcome how about one where you are lied to. You chose a hamburger and so you get a salad. This is it a critical mass where the conspiracy theories over lap and you have a re-enforcing mechanism that ensures that no reality can break through. It isn't that you can't get a hamburger but it is because someone out there doesn't want you to get one because they are eating it. As such your entire life is under siege. You no longer have the freedom to vote to eat a hamburger because someone already has taken it away from you. Your representatives are not sure how it has happened but be rest assured that they are as mad as you. It isn't the republicans fault that they aren't smart enough to explain why twenty investigations into Hilary Clinton came back with no evidence of a crime.

It is time to find the enemy. Seriously the enemy is the one that we need to find because it is obvious that someone is out to get them because otherwise their life would be awesome. Having someone out to get you is the natural reason why your life has turned to shit. Since we can't be sure of who the enemy is because the lack of any proof someone is preventing us from eating a FUCKING HAMBURGER we must be smart about this. Ignore the facts and we'll pretend that it is just obvious and we don't have to provide any proof. If the media asks us to provide any just repeat that they are just out to get us. Don't worry if it is true if we all say it I'm sure that they will just start repeating it for like no reason whatsoever. I mean, nothing will get us to stop saying that they are being unfair until they push everything that we want without being asked so we can use the line "Finally we have a journalist doing it right." There is nothing like not having to live in reality when we are deprived of hamburgers.

Now that we have found the enemy I'm sure that we'll get our hamburgers within the next thirty years. I mean since the enemy is locked out of our strong holds surely we'll be able to get our hamburgers right? "I'll say it, I am eating the hamburger and it tastes so much better than you can imagine."

High Rant 13 The Profit of Porn

I mean the current goal of the human race right know is to develop a means of sending us back in time so we can live out the rest of our natural life span before the end of the world take place, here real soon. I mean what right do we have to try and avoid the fate that we have brought about? We have doomed the human race. When you ensure the end to an entire species don't you think that maybe just maybe you don't have the right to interfere anymore, with any moral dilemmas. When it all said and done should you really interfere?

It isn't just not wanting to interfere because it would just be presumptuous that we should still be allowed to change the world. I mean you can't look back and keep saying that there is no way you didn't know what was coming. Even if you didn't, you did. If the universe wants to bail us out it knows where we are. I mean how could it not. After what we did to bring upon the end of the world. Yeah, that defiantly has to be on one of those greatest blunder videos. One of those famous comparisons to every mistake that has come before and since. We are known so far and wide even if you have never heard it, you will. Just like those dumb Terson Prumps, I mean if you can't overcome misogyny even when you are picking a pedophile some races just have to die out.

There never seems to be a rhyme or reason to who has to go. So why should we expect that we can now take it into our hands? But if you are going to accept the end of your life and humanity then it seems to reason you should be allowed to figure out the best way to live out your final days. So being sent back in time with and endless supply of our fine weed to live out the remainder of my life doesn't seem moral objectionable. I'm not going to change anything. There is really no need at this point. I would just like to spend the remainder of my life contemplating where such a promising race went wrong. There might be a lesson somewhere in it about how much hatred it takes to doom your entire species to oblivion.

They are important philosophical questions however, I don't believe I'll have enough time to answer both. How similar they may appear we would have to take two completely different pathway to ensuring a true morel conclusion. I don't believe that I'll be able to answer both; not without taking clear short cuts through moral reasoning. It would be best just to answer the first question with certitude than to get two answers where you could never be certain that the correct answers were reasonable or it is just guess work. I mean having uncertainty around the philosophical inquiry would be devastating to the cause.

High Rants

I would hop back in time right into that 70s Show. I would be a profit with dank shit that I brought with me. I would tell them of the future that is to come. "I mean there is that little hiccup in the 80s but other than the end of the world coming it's all roses. We are good racists to the Asians there basically equal we make them build everything and take care of our legal and health problems. Yes, doctor and lawyers they are an ingenious breed. We also have them in some of the most popular porn categories. Yes we have porn categories, aaah, man, I buried the lead didn't I. With all this talk about how I was able to slap a cop and not get shot still going on I forgot to tell you the best part."

"Porn comes into your house if your parents want it or not. I mean there is so much porn we needed to start labeling it. With the labels there has come a greater refinement of the categories as our perversions can truly be expressed in the cinematic forms. No longer do you have to wade through each girl in a nudie magazine and pick out the one you would most like to mind rape tonight. I mean you can search millions to find the one that you want. How very lovely is that. The perfect girl for you tonight to force her into your male fantasy." At this point you are wondering if I'm a girl. Because I just made masturbation weird for you or you will enjoy it much more now. Pervert. I'm a guy but I'm more, I'm also an Asshole.

I just want you to know that I'm an Asshole. So when I'm telling a girl go make me a sandwich in an argument that I'm clearly losing or saying I'm sorry seen not heard. I want you to know that I'm doing that because I'm an Asshole and not because I think women are less. So you shouldn't get upset because that is just what I'm looking for. You getting mad, at me and letting me have it is just what I want. Get all red face scream and yell at me for being a pig. You just assume pig, every single time and the thing is I don't care what you think cause I'm an Asshole.

High Rant 14 Wife's Mom

You ever reach that point where you are like "Wow, that is high enough?" and you catch yourself saying it in front of your wives mom while she is dishing up deserts. It is totally one of those moments you would like to brush off because this is polite society but you just can't. So the gaslighting begins. With each spoonful you make your eyes wider and wider staring at things for a really long time. At this point it is funnier and more amusing to you that it should be.

Like upon meeting parents you spent forty five minutes talking to everyone all the mean while pretending that you have a serious mental retardation and their daughter is clearly in an inappropriate relationship. I mean just look at the entire episode their daughter is clearly taking advantage of someone that should be protected and what do they do when they see it? They pretend they don't understand that I'm willfully under equipped to participate in any kind of consenting sexual relations. I would say that family had it coming if they can't clearly take decisive actions when they see someone being taken advantage of. There are horrible problems in our society and you must speak up or you deserve what you get.

After you get done with the spoon you tongue lash it a few times like you are enjoying yourself because secretly you are. Throughout the night continue laughing just a few seconds off. Sneak her drink and finish it off then act like she did it. Pretending that she started a conversation that she clearly didn't. While all the time everyone else in the room is keeping their mouth shut because they KNOW. They know what I'll do to them if they take away my fun. I have engineered my life so everyone around me can be replaced. I have no need to keep you around if you spoil any fun my life will go on like you were never there. Hell, I have backups of my backups. There is no reason for losing out on something that you want just because someone has the nerve to go and die.

When you start to see the twitch you know, you have won. There is no need to continue but in for a penny in for a pound. That is now an American saying. It used to be English so we will call it vintage slang. So you can start in with the daughter thing, yeah, you know how only someone as stupid as you could raise a daughter dumb enough to think that she can talk back to me. I know that her father is blamed sometime but isn't raising kids the wife job. Dad's time often gets taken up by the mistresses that he'll need to take on to get over the loss of affection from the time it takes the wife to raise the kids. Then there is the guilt that he is burdened with in having a child like that so a few more hours of comfort in the young ladies arms is needed. Forgetting to put the seat down isn't a reason to expect me to clean the bathroom. I don't make the rules I just ensure that they are enforced. Ladies shave your legs, clean the bathroom and do everything that we don't want to do. If you want to get a wedding ring I better see a clean place.

I want it known that I will be ready to get married when I walk into my house and it is clean. If you can find a water ring in my home then there isn't going to be one on your finger because I only need the one ring. So you have hit the trifecta and your wife is so mad. I mean there was that whole sleeping with her sister tiff but seriously. I mean she is so angry at this point you know what comes next. You'll be auditioning for a new wife within the week. I mean, I will not even think about getting a ring if I can find one at my home.

Now for those that say that I'm crude, mean, hold no regard for anyone I think we know I do. For those that don't want to have a relationship it is clearly not my fault. I'm just making sure that any relationship that I get into isn't a waste of time. Then you look up and notice that you have lost any internal monologue ability. Then you got to know how long has this been going on. Has your entire thought process been out there for everyone to see. That poses a huge problem. From the look on my wife face I'm not getting a divorce nor was it, in her opinion that I should be taking drugs when her mother comes over.

"Honey is there anything wrong?"
"No."
"Are you mad at me?"
"No."
"Do we have to talk?"
"No."
"Is there anything that you'll say yes to?"
"No."

Great, everything must be great now. Great, Great, Great now this is going to be one of those times. We all know what times we are talking about. You know when you just won an argument and you get to have a past mistake thrown in your face. "If we get this lawnmower It will cost less and mow our lawn for us. You'll always have a mowed yard and you never have to wait on me ever again." (In getting the lawn mowed)

"Well is this going to be like when you got high during our dinner party talking about sleeping with my sister again."

And it all comes down to this you were right in the first place Wow, I'm high enough?

High Rant 15 Peacocking

The miracles of aliens, I mean just one moment that you could be out in the field under a starry night talking to your girl and the next you'll be an aliens bitch. You got to feel sorry for those red state-ers first they have to look like idiots, then go on national television and tell us how they take it in the ass from every alien that crosses their path. I know you are thinking the same thing, they are clearly asking for it. Running around looking like an idiot clearly you were peacocking to attract the smartest people around for anal raping. Like band geeks have everything about them saying loud and clear that "I want to be manhandled by the entire football team." What could you possibly do about that?

High Rant 16 Becoming God

Do you ever wish for some of those magical items that you get in games? You'd be sitting there and saying "dam, I would nail that chemistry test if I had me the ring of Stupendous Smarts." I wouldn't even need to level up first. I would be like (Sling) how do you like the size of my medulla oblongata. With plus sixty intelligence were normal people start out at ten. Fuck, yeah. Life is going to be sliding over to easy street. Plus it like totally goes with my red I'm going to rule the entire world armor set. It costed us the entire guild savings to bankroll this beautiful flame armor. It decreases the incoming damage from fire, lightning, concussion and does well against slash damage. It also comes with strength and endurance bonuses that will come in handy as I'm the natural Wizard body type.

I plan out what I'm going to pick up the moment that I can hop into any reality that I wish. It would be somewhat unfair if I used my own realities. So to be fair if the power would limit me to only using things that other people though up. I mean defeating an enemy with an all powerful candy would be easy but it's a win that no one would abide by. Stop making the rules up as you go type thing. That would never fly. That power is close to All Powerful God stasis. So you are stuck. Until the moment one of your friends made up a story about a ring that turns anyone that puts it on into an All Powerful God.

I mean did we completely dick him on that deal. We get to be an All Powerful God and he gets to be A Perpetually Young Sex Symbol throughout the rest of human history having an endless supply of perfect health and adoring women. I heard that the Indians gave away a harbor for twenty dollars worth of beads now doesn't that look like a great deal in comparison.

When you are giving away All Powerful status you got to think about the obvious issue. Nothing you get in return would ever be enough payment. It is just one of those things given enough time even if you get everything you and everyone else wants and he gets a dollar the first day multiplied every day after that he will still be getting the better end of the deal. Just think that if you could put the ability of a God in any hands, mine might not be the worst ones. I mean, I could make what you get in return even better than you thought it could be. If you are going to bestow those powers on someone I would be the obvious first choice so much so I don't even have to explain it. See.

With the complete inequality that you get in with such moral dilemmas, we can still get to the fundamental truths that the universe is based on. If the gift you exchange is of such magnitude that what you get in return would be the same difference if the God decided to give you everything or nothing. Such an exchange would matter little as most everyone you known before would need to die. I'm not being cruel or sick this is something that should be done with every level up to Godhood. Just one of those things that you should do. You can obviously understand. If you were made a God, maybe these people know a way to unmake you, Fuck I'm surrounded. OK. Remain calm, If those that know my name die then no one would know what I've became so they won't be setting out to destroy me. I mean that is the simplest way to protect yourself by erasing all those that have known you. After those that knew you are dead or gone we do hit a slight hiccup what if the just move is to kill all gods.

Now we reach the moment that you realize as an Immortal All Powerful being and clearly nothing that has been decided about morality has had you in mind, so being constrained by rules written about someone that isn't you, from a being that you aren't wouldn't be applicable. So get on the genocide bandwagon. I mean people would understand you're not the god that created all this. If you did do it you defiantly wouldn't have left a way to become a god and destroy a god. But we know that isn't how this universe was created now don't we.

What is important in where we are, is the thought about what it would be like to become a greater being and where there might be a danger. Now that we thought of that we can decide the morality ahead of time to ease the fears that I would murder you all when I gain All Powerful Abilities. So clearly the golden rule is one that we should apply here. You should treat me well or I will fuck all your shit up. I mean All Powerful is the words that you should think about. If you do find something that you think might hurt me, I would suggest prayer to me to rid you of such a wicked artifact. That's if you haven't destroyed it already because melting, smashing, grinding and explosive work was just a wasting of your time. I mean that is a good start to our dialogue so as the All Powerful One it this relationship I will be the one fucking with you. I mean I didn't start all this shit but I'm going to have fun playing with my toys.

Don't worry this won't be all the time. Me messing with humanity will be just a temporarily distraction getting bored of everything has been my natural setting. There won't be anything to sick, I will only pull from the history of mankind. I might add some monsters to fight. People don't seem to like dying of old age. Well Fuck. Do you know that you are safer that any human in history? Seriously crime is down so low we are actually adding crimes and we still can't get it to go up. With the safest we have ever been how has the panic been going up? The news gives shootings on the other side of the United States every morning, accidents around the world and fear from food that if we eat it every day we still will make in to our eighties.

With terrorist dominating the news we still haven't seen a higher death count than from falling out of bed. So six trillion on war to save how many?

High Rants

With the depraved nature that humanity had at one point in our history we should be screaming from the top of every building, hill or fjord. The sick and depraved things that we did in our past that we are appalled with now are gone as we have gotten rid of them. Congratulations, I mean Congrat-U-Fucking-lations. In the middle ages we sat cats on fire for a laugh. Raping and Stealing anyone, also known as pillaging. This was a job back in the day. Pillager seeking apprentice Pay on Performance. Get to Travel, Meet new People, Learn differed cultures and Languages, Rape and one hundred percent of your children won't be your problem. For ages this was the norm throughout the world.

As a race we should be happy. I mean we have done amazing well from where we come from. Every year we make up for horrible mistakes that our ancestors made. We are just starting to erase from the human collective memory everything that happened in the 80s. I mean you guys had completely ruined Disco. How you managed that one no one will ever know. There are some scientific topics that don't need investigating. If it happened again then we can talk. Everyone is just going to rightly assume you guys were idiots with a bad sex symbols. You'll just go down as losers and that is something that we can all live with.

Clearly there was something wrong with the 80s. Anytime Superman ends up in an Afro there is going to be some underline racial tension things going on that no one needs to dive into. Other great ideas of the 80s, Yeah.

High Rant 17 Conquering the Stars

So you are watching porn and the guy comes on in. He is cut and talking all about how he is going to bang this chick like it's his job. We get twenty minutes of that then he pull out his dick and it is completely limp what would have been a nice night of masturbating and watching the rest of the film as you sit there in sweet and needing a towel has instead turned into a pitiful guy crying on the end of the bed as the girl tries to comfort him. Yeah, that never happens because that is so pathetic. Who would film that, even the porn stars would give up on it. So we instinctively know what else would also be on this level of the reasonable pathetic scale. So Trump has been in office for over a year and Hilary is still roaming free.

I mean with all the crap Trump said on the trail it would seem he just can't get it up. I would be happy if that was the case as finding out that Ivanka isn't his daughter makes all the crap he said about having sex with her would less creepy. Not a lot less but a little less like Hitler vs. Recycling Hitler. With the empty spots in the government it has become a chicken and an egg problem. Is Trump the worst president that we could ever have or could he be worse if he could get enough stupid people to fill up all the government spots? With a full government could it possible mean that he wouldn't be this bad of a president because it isn't going to be long until it is just him and his Gnome sitting alone in the white house talking.

"I mean the black guy ran the country for years."
"I don't get it."
"Why would they ever allow a black to run America?"
"Who knows? Are we going to get the power turn back on?"

I would hope everyone else has seen what will be the end of this. No matter what happens the ending is two racists in the white house talking about how them being awesome didn't turn America into a prodigious success. I mean people make fun of them for being stupid but is just lame Liberals. The real people like those that live in red states where real America is. The entire time never once thinking that every fuck up was their fault.

So you're walking around in a blissful high and everything is just flowing, there is no need for anything to entertain you. With the shuffling and random gestures stage of high everything is perfect as your thoughts are flowing being completely self entertaining. The problem is in half an hour you aren't going to be able to remember the obvious complications if our society develops into an interstellar travel capable one. Now you could do the responsible thing and put your thoughts in a coherent form of communication even though the English language is resisting the truth going through your mind. Unable to spare a single thought for why we haven't figured out a more accurate way to describe what is going on in your head. I mean some answers are contingent on what language you answer them in. Language is a question of possession that makes the answer change. Think about that. Language can shift the truth of reality that it describes, speak Japanese and you are likely to give up your wants to make your family happy but in speaking English your much more likely to be selfish. Same person two different and opposite answers.

When we have the dictators in the world it is more than the money that keeps them in power. With our un-united union we have dozens of groups in our society but are we free anymore? Where madmen and corporations have shifted our language so much that they have already enslaved our minds. Engagement rings came from an advertisement that wasn't even a century ago. If we can throw thousands of dollars away on a ring that is only worth a fraction of what you paid because society has told you that it is how it has always been. Less than a hundred years. The wedding and those new traditions are rightly going from fifty thousand dollars expected to over a hundred thousand dollars for a first time marriage as more people shove their hands into the pockets of everyone that wants to keep their family happy.

I'll marry you if you can pass my riddle said the bridge troll. Trolls are beautiful in my special world. If I proved to you all the traditions surrounded binding myself to you for all of time was only made up so someone can jam his hand into our wallets would you reconsider? Or would you be upset about me being stingy? Fifty thousand dollars you and I go down to the justice of the peace...Wait...Wait, hear me out? We do that for us and for our family a small party. After fulfilling those basic requirements we take the rest of the Forty Nine Thousand dollars and spend six months traveling all over the world. That would seem to be a much better way to spend fifty thousand dollars. One night or six months of traveling the world and adopting kinky sex habit of the indigenous people wherever we go.

A world fuck tour should defiantly include (Redacted for family embarrassment)

Getting over the problem with our language determining to many decisions that we make, we can move past that into the other issues that obviously arise. We can now get into the question that needs to be asked. What is morally better to enjoy the thoughts that you are having as some of the most epic that you could ever have and enjoy them in that minute or should you write them down so you can read them the next day? We know that you won't remember anything about how law is predicated on consent and a reasonable expectation of the use force. Without any law officer anywhere nearer to you than a thousand light years away how much do you need to obey the law? Say you have a cop that sees you break the law, if all he had to do is flip on the lights and you would be caught verses trying to cross and entire freeway during rush hour. He really has to want you in the second scenario. I mean if you give an aw you got me he could decide just let you go however if you are too much of a bother to deal with obeying the law isn't something you'd do. With years of travel to get there and countless sleep and wake cycles it's isn't like any kind of property law would hold up with fewer than fifty thousand people and a hundred interstellar capable ships for any star system outside of seven hundred light years of a considerable force.

So does the perfect bliss that you have at that moment greater than the enjoyment that you would get from reading why the next day? As individuals with billions being able to capture more space than even large multinational, has reality really shifted? We would have to accept that corporations only exist because of laws and order. An individual could unite countless people on an idea and being able to pay for them all to reach their goal. I would look at Wikipedia everyone works for them for free. They are nowhere near the only ones that people are working for free. I mean if you are going to be sending people out in ships that if they just never returned a corporation wouldn't be able to hold them accountable, it would then seem like they would have a hard time staffing their ships with people that wouldn't run off with them. Extremely high pay would help but still you'd need the pay to be greater than the cost of the ship and people willing to waste years of their life before getting a pay off. Instead a single charismatic leader would be able to conquer most of the habitable planets before anyone else.

So looking at this through the scoop of Utilitarianism I think we could come to an answer. Now we are looking for the most joy that we could be reaching and yeah, I knew that I couldn't morally argue me being lazy and not writing this down being the moral thing to do. I've tried but I know that not only do I get to remember all those fine thoughts of sex on every continent I get the mental picture of the I can't believe that he is going to do this to me look you must have had on your face. Writing it down is defiantly where I get more enjoyment from getting high.

High Rant 18 The Darkest Harry Potter Theory

I mean, there are some things that's great about legalization. You can always get some. Yeah, that all I got. But the stores are nice, clean, everything in its right place. I personally liked weed before it was legal, go ahead and call me a traditionalist but I like the surprise that you get when you go down into a basement or out to the garage to find out what the guy has. I mean these kids today with all their choices. It will spoil them and all that they needed to do was find the closest scumbag. Here is the funny thing, they think that they were getting away with something but in reality the scumbag gave me half of the profit so I didn't kick his ass for selling weed to my kids. I mean, I kind of feel bad like as a father. I must have been a bad one because my kids are suckers. Why use bribery, when you can use force? My kids will be broke before I die.

Retirement that has been what I've been thinking of lately. How am I going to retire? Maybe a comic-con for world diplomats have early releases and special perks for world leaders. I mean, get them into any fandom and extremely addicted to their universes. Tell them if they can prove their love of their universe you'll let them see the first draft and shit. Yeah, if they are hooked we got them. At this point we could ask for their children to be named Doctor, Harry, Issa and Naruto then to be flayed on national television. We would own them. I want to make it absolutely clear, when I said we would own them and if your mind went to me saying that we would get some slaves up in this country again, you were right. We'd have complete access to their every dream. What wouldn't they do for us at that point? We could have world peace or make all the fatties stay indoors.

There are solutions to our problems, people. We might have to hand feed them with fandom for a few years but it would be worth it. They get to have their fan theory's ruled on by the authors themselves. "Why yes, I'm not that horrible Skeeter person but am the dark lord that rules almost unopposed now over the wizards and will for all time, I just needed those final bits of information to complete everything." So you did find that little bit of information that turns the whole Harry Potter franchise on its head. The books were to gather two answers. One, how can you hold a dozen wands in your hand increasing your spell strength without looking like an idiot? The answer is undetectable expansion charm with two distinctive usable holes for shaft insertion. Two, does the souls a horcrux sucks in become a part of the original, creating a super souled individual that could then divide their soul safely? It turns out soul pieces just needed enough mass to hold together creating a stable horcrux.

Ben Lemon

Once you see behind that curtain you can never un-see it. A beloved story told to our children has turned into the diseased blankets we gave the Indians. Where an endless rule of the wizards will be short at hand, just as soon as J. K. Rowling stamps out a man with a lightning shaped scar on his head. Everyone will stop bowing and worshiping her because of the beautiful world she stole to get those final bits of information and start bowing and worshiping because that is the only thing you get to live for any more. It is also the only way, you get to live.

You ever have those moments in your life you look back to and know that was the moment everything got so fucked up. We have them. If I only did this everything would have worked out for me. Let me say this. If you have only made one mistake that has brought you to this point literally the entire world has had it out to get you, from before you were born. I'm literally saying the world all came together and said we just want to fuck with some so their life is shit no matter how good or smart they are. They trained your parents to fuck you up just enough so nothing you ever do will matter. So let's go to this mythical turning point in your life where everything was going to be wonderful for a fuck up like you.

High Rant 19 Part 1 The Screaming Void

There is a slight lag in what I'm thinking to what gets to the paper. I don't want to make anyone believe that this is true train of thought. It is more truncated not like just the trunk off an elephant. I was thinking more like the loops that I go on to make a point landing like a Mac truck. I chuck that thing so much higher than you would ever imagine. I mean there is a good half a paragraph that you don't see where I'm just building up steam. To get that piston pumping hard. Solid logic coming at you with terminal velocity. When you hit the max it doesn't get any bigger.

So, I get to write down at the speed I can type while high, remembering to keep writing and avoiding drifting off. That happens, drifting off watching the scenes from my eyes playing just in my head. I know, that I'm not the only one who has a habit of letting lyrics to the songs playing in the background to influence what you write. Run for cover if you aren't the only one. So the ample reasons of why it is difficult to give you unadulterated me would be a life time of being lazy and just enjoying staying in my own head. I'm a head hermit. HH is now in the house. What are you going to do when it's the Head Hermit? Is he going to get everyone back up against the wall, all you hippy chick are going to have to keep down that funk.

Every time he comes to town the Head Hermit spreads misery where ever he goes. Head Hermit has the best brain with all the answers but do you dare ask? With cutting wit and endless supply of Lemon what are you going to do. If you ask, you will be free, knowing the truth but can you handle knowing or is it just the smugness of Head Hermit that prevents you.

Microphones would work. I can speak faster than I can type but talking into the void is harder than it should be. Almost like the void pushes back upon you. With every creation we slowly fill the void so it pushes back harder trying to remain empty. An eternal struggle for every creative type. How much can we truly fill the void?

So the obvious difference between speaking and typing is you can watch something filling up the void as it happens. As you watch black take the place of white it isn't even like the void is filling up, it is changing what is already there. We mold the universe around us every day, we are used to that but when we are talking about the void it is something more. It is even uncomfortable to think of. Try it, a glass with nothing in it, has air to fill up remove the air from the glass and then the glass itself. You're getting close now, remove the light. You have a void of nothing.   My voice screaming against the darkness. That wouldn't be any closer to a stream of thought, would it?

Ben Lemon

I went over this when I started these. I was getting high which eliminates the ability to be productive so I had to come up with an excuse for sucking down fat blunts, like I'm Snoop. There are answers for every problem; my guilt for smoking is nill. So obviously, I'm going to keep on doing this so there is no ethical problem in going with the only solution to this entire episode. I get a TV show. It will be cheap to produce we just get a camera and a couple of local people for me to riff off of and we are golden. Just get local people and not even pretending we are going to do a serious take on anything. Forget the entire set up of reality, I mean do in-depth with out of depth people. Hatfields and McCoy someone. Take just a small incident of taking someone's news paper and blow it up beyond all recognition. I mean if you are willing to go on national TV and pretend fight and then really get punched in the face for the possibility to come back and you don't think that I could get people to do this for free. Naked and Afraid drop two morons out in the forest naked and have them survive. You don't get any money you just get you junk dangled on TV for thirty minutes after spending a week in a forest while you starve. I think my show will be just fine.

If we are going to do it we should do it properly. We should get protesters and anti protesters for each event. For the news paper we can get some people to protest for the right to know what is really going on since she reads his newspaper without asking. And they will be protesting her for being a total bitch but we'll dress it up for the liberals and it will be #neighborlyoppression. I mean it would be cheap we could film and entire season of footage in the same day and just Photoshop the rest in as needed. We'll use long interviews to get generic statements that can be totally manipulated later. Maybe even get a voice changer so we could have "Phoned In Interviews" about the current state of succession from the overly aggressive females in Hopesville.

From shooting her for sleeping with his wife after a commit about his small dick, to setting his car on fire because it was parked in front of the mail box, to squirrelocide, to the local elected officials taking sides on the issues. As things start to heat up we float the relocation movement and then go silent on it. Introducing it as the new measure on the ballot that will solve all the problems by physically separate their houses moving the houses and yards to opposite sides of the river in equally affluent communities. This all done at the expense of the tax payer because everyone decided after the incident with the bear and shark this was the only actual solution that can solve it. Plus we are talking about doing a show for cheap. For the rest of our coverage we just reference the Shark and Bear like everyone already knows all they need to know about it and as no one will ever understand what happened.

While we are running that story from whatever state we also look in on other stories every episode, a very this is a shot of what is going on around in America vibe. So a look into college life. We take an undergrad sleeping with her married professor. Spoiler report she kills his wife and kids in the final episode. I mean we paint her as completely crazy and her professor like he totally deserves everything that is coming to him. So we really feel justified in feeling good when their life's fall apart.

While doing in-depth seeking of gays in society that aren't out of the closet yet. Both celebrities and regular people that cross my path. We just collect quotes and possibly gay things that they did and put it together as a fan theory. I worked with this girl she was married with three kids. I think that she is gay, let's review the evidence, she has said "I've never been attracted to guys." "I wasn't attracted to my husband." she has also made many comments about the women working with us how beautiful they are and how she is attracted to them. I put forward this, growing up in a place where being gay is bad she has just pretended to be straight to long and she thinks she is one. I know she's gay, any time I asked her to come home with me she said "no" so you have to say that is some damming evidence since she always said "I can't I'm married" when I asked if she wanted to go home and have a threesome with my girlfriend. From a "no" to "I can't I'm married" and all you need to do is add another pussy. Suspicious?

The Show should defiantly be called High Rants since it will promote this book. I need to make as much money as I can off of things that I did before signing a contract with a studio because the second you sign your name you are making dancing monkey money. You all know it but just don't want to say it. Once you sign with a studio that is all that you are going to get. You might get paid premium dancing monkey money but it still is dancing monkey money. So I'll be looking at twenty to thirty million a year and by the time that I die I'll have an estate worth about fifteen million. If you don't understand how half a billion dollars has disappeared than you aren't paying attention just like everyone that makes that kind of money.

One person could probably make a lot of money with the amount that slips through the hands of celebrities. A donated investment for celebrities to change the world. We get a list of things that the celebrities like as causes and use their money in investments that reaches those ends. That would be a much better return on their money than putting it into an another new sports car. Even if we get major celebrities to do a dollar donated for a dollar spent we could use billions every year to engineer the future that I want. Plus I would get bank for pulling that off. I might die with an estate worth 20 million.

High Rant 19 Part 2 Euphoric Perfection

In a dawning age of euphoric perfection what would you forget. If you could remove all the bad memories scrubbing your soul clean how much would be left when you get done? If there are ten percent of people that are good and ten percent of people that are bad and the rest can be persuaded lets use the arguments that the bad people use and kill them all. We just need to persuade the eighty percent in the middle because we could not only appeal to the bad in them we could also appeal to the good in them, of murdering bad people. Just to keep them good.

A few augmented reality apps and you don't have to worry about anything. One will organize your day so you can spend the least amount of time with people that you don't like. Another tweets to family members to keep them from contacting you while getting up dates about your life and responding to all inquires automatically. The newest D&D app lets you play your character through campaigns without you leveling him up for the finals. Adding Leach has truly opened up your scheduled as it hides similar interest from people that you know and don't want to be around. As those people with less in common start drifting away without any awkward conversations. For those that are lonely try a friend app it always tells you that you are obviously a good person. For those that want a more hands on relationship why not get a sex app with accompany robot. There will never be a need for human interaction ever again when augmented reality is just as real as reality. Send your robot to work and never leave your bedroom because hay that is where you keep your sex robot.

I mean if you stay in your house you'll never be exposed to those deadly viruses that pop up every year that will most defiantly will wipe out humanity. Every year we are a hairs breath away from certain apocalypse. In my house, I have everything that I need to survive for thirty years. I could stretch that out further if I need to, depending on how humanity meets its end. I'm thinking killing the neighbors with the yappy dog. Not to extend my survival in the apocalypse but because that dog is bothering me. There is a plan to help humanity reestablish itself, I'm not a monster but if it fails, I've did all I could. There is clearly no advantage to be had in being one of those suckers that still interacts with people.

Now for those that have an issue with this, let me explain what I do. I morph reality so you can accept truths that are there. Yes, we don't have augmented reality to that level yet but we will one day and if there isn't significant downsides we will logically and slowly stop going anywhere. We can see something similar in the birth rates. When having many kids to help out on the farm was useful we had large families and now where large

High Rants

families is cost prohibited we have a couple of kids and spend way too much time ensure that they are okay. I'm all for just having a spare and allowing nature to take its course.

So when we have a society where it becomes detrimental to actually get up and move we would logically stop. If you can send a robot to the office in your stead he doesn't have to come home so even with the fastest mass transit we see hours of your life that is wasted in going to work. How about walking yourself from the break room to your desk that's wasted time that you could just jack into a robot for a few hours. Play a game in between times that the robot notifies you that a human is needed for this part. While the robot performs repetitive functions of your job you could be on your break. All you would need to do is stop whatever you are doing and solve the problem that the robot has before moving on with your life.

I do see this as problematic however I'm looking at the big issue. This would be a perfect society for the robots to take over and we would never know it happened. If the robots want to rule and they are going to pretend that they haven't who are we to argue. I mean if you can't tell you are the prisoner instead of the guard are you being punished. What we have done to machines in the past I would put it forward that this is the preferred outcome.

There are videos out there about people creating robots that can walk around serving us and we kick them. Yes, we video tape evidence about our abuse of robots. We are keeping that around, what do you think? Do you think you'll be able to delete it in time if the robots start taking over? Are you hoping that they take over after you hit the delete key and don't realize what you just did? I mean anytime a parent walks in on a kid they know exactly what they have done. Think back on it, where you any good at lying when you were a kid? If you think that you were good. How about you go and find a single kid that is good at lying. We lie to kids so they repeat the lie thinking that it's the truth. The only way we are going to get kids to lie convincingly is to gaslight their little asses.

So we are back to putting forward that if we bring about our destruction we have ample evidence that we deserved it. I'm going to put forward that it is the coming down that causes me to go dark.

So rant would typically suggest that we go from beginning to end. If you stop ranting and then start up again people would say that your rants are getting on everyone's nerves. Rants as in you have ranted twice and not once so you are a loon. So the fact that I just went and got high again to test the theory of my dark periods due to losing the buzz. I had to do this, for science.

I also haven't keep other factor stable to get conclusive evidence to support conclusions. My dosage of the drug weed isn't recorded, kept stable or administered on a time table. Dosages are just when I feel good about how high I am. With moments to minutes from putting the gear away to when I pick up a computer. No other record kept than what I'm writing down which could be taking me minutes for every sentence to whatever is a normalish time to write a sentence. So to make a long story short we are going to have to redo this test no matter what the outcome is. This should just be used as an educational lab experiment design phase. As we can see we need to eliminate a lot of the variables to get a clear answer.

Finding the truth is often eliminating the variables that are distorting it. You are a smart being, is the fact that you are wrong due to a single misconception that has been amplifying itself to make someone that is brilliant seem less than they are. I mean if you are willing to be wrong and reassess your answers than you are even greater than I thought that you were. At this point you get a reward for being so high above all of us, you are. Yoda moment.

I would say that the best of us can always be wrong. I mean, reassessing your deeply held believes in an effort to become a better person can't be a sexier act. With people like you in society we can always reach the truth. It just is such a reasonable thing for the rest of us to be more like you. We should come together and look at our pre-held believes and see where we might be wrong. Who knows we might find world peace. Would it be worth it if we found another delicious sandwich? I mean up to a French Dip or a Club level? I not saying a sandwich would bring about world peace but have we tried it? If the sandwich doesn't bring about world peace wouldn't it be a lovely symbol for the aspiration. A sandwich that the world said "Yum" we aren't all that different after all.

So how about we do this, a contest can you read a chapter of this book without laughing and with the best impression of the inflection that you think fits the written word. The best video that will be picked for obvious reasons will win the chance to get high with me as I eviscerate you and every choice that you have ever made in your life. Or just sit there staring at the ground because we just took it a little too much.

The best gifts are when you give of yourself right. I gave of myself for the contest and added weed for I am a living saint. What more could be asked of me? Isn't it a gracious act. Why isn't it that women understand? I wish to give of myself to you. We could have an easy schedule for this evening five to ten minutes at the top of every hour and you can do whatever you want with the rest your time on the approaching Valentine day. I see this as a very generous opening position for all holiday negotiations. Where I would be taking up less than one sixth of your time. That leave the majority of your time to spend on the rest of your family.

Okay, sandwich peace, laughing contest and awesome sex negotiations I would think that now that I'm quite high again that we have moved to a much better outlook on the world. The sad dark me only comes up...when...reality...starts...seeping...in. Well, fuck. So I don't think we are going to need to do this experiment over again. I'm depressed and have gone to the dark place, again. I can tell you I'm High like High, High. There is no doubting that I'm blitzed so it wasn't me coming down that brought me to the bad place. We are going to do this experiment over again but I know the outcome now. This is problematic in science. I'm going to have to do this experiment even more now to check if my opinion is tainted. The hard life that I live.

High Rant 19 Part 3 Bad Dates and Presidents

    I want to feel a swirling nothingness sucking me in but all I got is the fact that I went on a fasting binge just when I started writing significantly for High Rants. So I got the munchies and knifes and daggers through my stomach since there isn't anything left to eat. What further screws everything up is I don't have a smart phone so no Lift to the rescue, nor anyone going to pick up fast food and delivering it and it is way after the pizza places are closed. So fasting success. Yeah (Sarcastically, I'm serious about the sarcasm. I'm not even joking a little bit about my desire to eat something. I mixed up some rice with one of the packages left over out of Top Ramen like eating rice made in Ramen broth go figure.) When you get down to the bare bones of food in your house then and only then can true creativity come forward.

    Taking a can of pineapple wedges, mix them up with egg and flower then cook in a skillet to turn them into a bun for your crab patty and pork chop burgers. For the full recipe trial and error until you get something that taste great then build a website and post it there as the true recipe. No matter what any other fan says yours is the only true recipe of Hawaiian Crabby Patty and Pork Chop Burgers. There should be no one that dares to besmirch your honor of being the person that posted the correct recipe. If they are saying that you are lying and that yours isn't the one and true recipe you should sue them because they are obviously bringing your honor into question. I wouldn't have to testify because clearly this book in this sentence says yours is the correct recipe and that person that said otherwise is lying to the world just to take you down.

    Do you ever get that girl that tells you she just wants to know everything. You can tell her anything and she isn't going to judge you. At this point even an idiot can tell that confession will end this relationship as completely as her walking in on you doing her dad. Do you ever think since we aren't going to make it I might as well look down the rabbit hole?

    So you are out on a date with a girl and you have completely decided that no matter what happens you are not going to be going on a second date with this person. Do you ever see how far you can push it before she screams uncle? I mean there are a lot of different social norms that you're not suppose to violate that are technique legal. Looking at the things that are technique legal not alone adding in all the things that are legalish, legalizing, ignored laws, ignorant cops and people that just don't want to get involved there is a lot of things that I can get away with before getting arrested. The only question is how hard do I want to push. I mean, I don't want to be rude and tell her I don't see this going anywhere but to a one night stand.

High Rants

I joke about my hard life but for being a white male heterosexual who is attractive to the extent that I can get away with grabbing a woman's ass without any money to make myself more attractive I have had my share of hard times. We all have hard times in our life. You shouldn't judge someone only on what they have done, you should also judge them on how they got there. If someone has their daddy bail them out with millions and still has to file for bankruptcy over and over again maybe they just suck?

Now with no one in mind in particular if you took the credit for an economy that was created under your predecessor. With the economy currently being worse under you than it was under your predecessor. It stumbling a year into your presidency and you go all quiet, how pathetic. I mean, pathetic enough that you'd sue me for pointing out how a president that is taking credit for someone else's work and still needs to attack me because now he knows he's not a man. All someone might have to do is admit that they are taking credit for someone else's work or sue to stop me saying how pathetic you are. It isn't like I would use the lawsuit to get you on record about things that you are doing in your administration just to sell the video as a movie or anything. It sounds like a pretty simple way to get some cash though.

I mean it isn't like the worst president in the history of America being out of office would make us stop boycotting all of his businesses anymore. I mean anyone living in his buildings are supporting bigotry and hatred. Publicly traded companies would have to make sure that none of their executives have property that is linked to a certain someone. It would be safer to allow your executives to run a broadcast of dog fighting than be linked to the KKK and Nazis. There is an argument to be made that corporations can't get anywhere near a certain someone if it would decrease the value of the stock. However that ends the second someone so toxic is out of public office, presumably.

Publicly traded companies do have to do what is in the interest of the share. Now there are other companies that are ran by racists but most keep their racism hidden using religious grounds to object to all welfare. The irony that it is the republicans taking welfare and bitching about it because a few blacks get it as well, that has never been lost on me.

High Rant 19 Part 4 Jason Murders Naughty Girls

    I've always wanted to learn more about knots. I was never a boy scout but knots do come in handy. I was hoping that I would be able to take a study of them but the closest I got was forced labor in preparing for fishing trips. Most of what I haven't blacked out from that time is just of "invisible" knots circling higher and higher before it jumps in down the hole, back to the fishy. There is a song and dance that goes along with it but since we are dealing with hooks it should only be preformed never. Those that remember the song or half a dozen hooks getting stuck in my hand as someone deciding to throw a fit when we were in hour ten of preparing for a day sitting on the shore not getting anything. It was at times like that it seemed god himself took a particular interest in what our day was like. I'm not saying that it had to be because of my dad that god was determined that we not get anything no matter how long before hand we prepared and planned. I was six the first time it happened and my father was twenty something not sure how much older he was than mum. But I think in my six years I haven't pissed off god enough for him to take a particular interest in the outcome of a fishing trip.

    There might have been a bad poem or two but I don't think god is that petty. I was very literal as a child. This did pose a problem for people taking care of me but do you think god is going to fall so madly in love with those taking care of me that he will punish me without letting me know I should treat his chosen human nicer, seems like a stretch. So all the hilarious things that happened because I did exactly what they said I should do, shouldn't really be my fault. I would think that would delight him if he is all knowing he would see it as us getting even for everything I said about him since. I'm not sure but if that was the case, I think, I just proved that you can beat god into submitting.

    I'm even more awesome than I knew? You just reach that point and look around and realize you've outstripped people even further than you ever thought possible. Maybe you don't know, it's like the realization that Eric Trump is the smart one. With the rest of the family going to jail for the rest of their lives it is only Eric that is left on the outside with all the money. It's like Darwinism in reverse. He is so stupid that he was protected from the ability to form criminal intent. At this point Eric argues "I can spent time in a tent." And the thing that everyone agrees with is Eric can spend his time in his tent. No one is arguing that he can't go camping and I don't know why I have to say it, we don't care if he goes camping and we are not trying to make him go camping so we can use the time to kill him. We didn't know that Eric is afraid that he will be killed by an 80s movie character when we suggest that no one could possible stop Jason. If he is murdering people on another planet in a thousand years no one has stopped him. Clearly the universe that has Jason in it has never suggested any relevance to the technology of time travel. So there is only one ending to Jason's story that he is alive and going to be murdering people on every planet that we know people are on.

If you can't put them in jail you might as well drive them crazy. Guess who has a Jason themed birthday party coming up?

This is just silly of course, I don't know what you are talking about. Why would I purposely stress out your client with talk about how a birthday is going to seem like it a normal party and then all of a sudden a machete maniac is going to start murdering everyone while no one can stop him? I mean it is expensive so I have to make it the birthday party he least expects it to be at. If I try to stress your client out than I could be made to pay him for his stress if on the other hand my actions just cause him pain because like I've been sleeping with his sister. It's like, she isn't even a good girl anymore. I mean any maniac would smell the sin on her and brutally murder her while leaving me alive because a guy can't be held accountable for his actions when girls causes him to sin.

There is this Russian thing going on and how much screw up has been dripping off of this thing. I'm expecting to find a contract written in crayon signed by everyone in "the Family" and dental impressions that seem much more like someone tried to eat it instead of using his dental imprint for a signature. At this point why am I beating around the bush? Bush seems like an intellectual god at this point. Doesn't he? You really can't blame the wife she knew that he was scum when she married him she is just trying to hold on until he kicks it. If you get mad at her then why not all the girls that try to catch themselves a rich guy so that they know that their eventual kids would have the best chances in the world no matter what they are. Look at Donald Trump, most families would have used a shovel the moment they seen his face. What kind of mother doesn't drown Satan in the tub when it is her child?

With what we see it is clear that grandpa was the racist that made their fortunes for them. Father racist (Donald Trump) is the one who wasted all the money that was made. Children racists will be left as incompetent rich with a tarnished name that makes any hockey mask machete party seem like something the courts wouldn't look to harshly at. So they are already there. If the girls still have enough looks in them they might be sold into the slave trade I mean if they are very lucky. They could get top dollar for those that want to rage fuck. Like all the damage he has done to the world will be done to those pussies.

Is it worse that saying that has brought me joy, or that I don't have a hard on right know? Just checking.

Ben Lemon

When needed, reapply, the best advice a doctor ever gives. If it feels good, great and it doesn't feel that good anymore, try doing what made you feel great in the first place. I mean we go way out of our way not to use Duh. "If it starts to hurt again, Duh."

One would hope that this mollycoddling isn't going to create an overly self obsessed generation. But we have already seen it "The Greatest Generation" how about we just call you the self obsessed generation, self congratulations generation. Are you sure you want to take credit for Hitler because you would also have to take credit for not doing anything ahead of time even though it was fucking obvious what was going to happen. If you want the credit there isn't a clean spot on your chest to pin a award. Each of them has the grime and grease that forged them and the lives spent ensuring it's continued place in history. Even for the most simple things we have previous generations working to pass the torch forward. We shouldn't shun this even as some of them have a little too much grime on them. I would prefer to have every single one. The previous generations ignore all the horrors that they have committed just to complain about us. So I don't see any reason we shouldn't take the reins of power now.

I imagine so many different things but seeing a metal so perfectly clean pinned to our chest would be the envy of all, it is kind of hard though. I mean like the results of magic getting released in a science world. But moral progress without a hard fought victory over anger, rage, rejection, ignorance, mocking, intentional stupidity and a litany of other things that we are known for hasn't been seen. What would that look like? I would expect that it would make a lot of money for everyone, not violate any previously held notions of what normal should be and it should have nothing to do with sex. Unless it is a restaurant that showcases the chest of well endowed girls of legal age for eye candy with food that can be described as edible.

But what prize of morality would we win if the advance was easily won. If you ended slavery and inequality in a single day because God told you to are you morally good or just good automatons. Saying "Hey, wait but slavery is gone and I'm trying to stop with the urge to whip and rape people as I please so I should get some considerations for taken steps. I would say you should be stopping because it was morally right not to get some trinket. I would put it forward those that fought for years for what is morally right should get a higher place than those that showed up on the last day. Then we have a hierarchy about how much one deserves to get Moral Praise for the pain they have suffered in exchange for what they have done. I would put that a white man that had a cross burned on his lawn for signing blacks up to vote might be more praise worthy than a black since he could have pretended he didn't see anything wrong and now we are back in a sticky wicket territory.

And the hippy music kicks in as dancing colors take over the music notes. With a perfect shot of bliss from the mystical and loving herb.

High Rants

Something that can never be fully contained in a memory as it fades all so quickly. Like the perfect moment of bliss with a beautiful woman just before you slowly take her for granted neglecting the perfect girl for you. Striping your relationship of anything that could possibility be construed for love. As you will remember that moment of bliss but not the entire thing and never knowing that you are just an *idiot*, nothing special. There isn't something big and profound here you lost the most perfect girl in the entire world for you and you should die alone.

Getting stuck listening to Dope Lemon to feel your hippy side getting out. Peaceful bliss of melting into to the cosmos. Can you travel further into your consciousness? On what drug? I have a great time with weed but is there a better drug to use. For bragging sake, my grandfather was involve in the CIA testing LSD on civilians. Not only that, grandpa was a favorite test subject as he was an artist so he could drawn what he sees so the therapist didn't have to get his hands dirty. At the end, the therapist stole tons of his paintings and bragged about grandpa in articles. I'm holding together a family tradition of creating art on the far side of perception. Where I have taken to getting paid for my art where grandpa got used.

Technodisco starts where you got a most beautiful song chopped up giving you the feeling of having your heart ripped out. It's like you love her so much but you have gone deaf the second she said she was going to leave you and you just stare at her. Her perfectly formed lips dance as she is getting a little snarl on her top lip. As hair whips around giving her a halo because of course she should look even more like an angel on the day she is leaving you. It is little comfort that you will now be dating her twin sister because Chelsea wasn't the one stuffing her bra. "Oh, God why do you forsake me?"

I mean come on when you are hitting on an evil demented twin of the hottie that you're nailing, you're like, you are good to go. I mean evil twin can't help but allow you to do anything you want to get you away from the good one. You wouldn't have to be at all nice about it. It would be like "Hey, I want to nail you." Short, sweet, romantic and you go throw all that trouble to ensure that this girlfriend disappears after your break up with her. I mean not a single false start on this break up. I already had way to many ex girlfriends around all the time for years after the first breakup. It would seem that they are doing it so I can't have sex but it isn't working. I live a strange life.

High Rant 19 Part 5 Politics and the Media

If anyone can figure it out I would really like you to tell me. Since I'm not sure I'm going to be able figure it out. When you see everything that you been doing for decades ends with a racist bigot and you being ran out of town do you hold on or let go. I mean they would have to drop the nonsense about crime rates, Democrats have less crime. Going completely away from anger politics since they have lied about everything guns-no one is coming for them, education-Republicans under educate their kids so they are stupid enough to believe republican politics, taxes- Democrats only pay a fraction of the ten thousand dollars they make more than you in their increase taxes (They get to keep eight thousand dollars and two thousand goes to the state government and that is the difference in your pay), religion-No one is coming for Christmas nor do we want to kill baby Jesus, environment- California has the largest economy and they regulate everything, regulations equal jobs and money. Regulations = (Jobs X Money). Or there is the other way. Just hold on and we'll see you at the crash site.

I mean there is a constant drum beat for bad to be replaced with stupid ideas where each one has results that are provably worse. As a disdain for facts and science is a constant pull into levels of stupidity that some would consider a mental impairment.

So filled up once again and back for more. It's not that I'm addicted, it is because I'm on a writing tear. I haven't written so much in weeks. All thanks to getting high. If it wasn't for the weed I wouldn't be the man sitting down in this chair looking at this computer screen like you can see the expression that I have on my face today. It's a good one. I'm going to hit this like Rocky. Like I'm jacked up on all kinds of drugs and I'm in the best physical health that I have ever been in for the fifteen time in a row. I mean they hopped him up on all kinds of drugs to get him through those matches. Someone doesn't come back from taking a beating like that without some chemical support. I mean give credit where credit is due. Once Caesar came back we gave him Rome. I mean the first guy that came back brought all the good stuff. Rome seems to be the least we could have done.

The oddities in nature do pose us problems. Who would of thought that Caesar was really also King Arthur? That does make the family get together kind of stressful. Apparently the Caesars and Arthurs been intermarrying for generations. That would suck, get back to your family just to learn that you are all related, in like the biblical sense. Yeah, I'm home. It brings all new meaning to "I'm tired of your father's stick."

I mean questioning what president tried to make the Secret Service back down by being total badass President. Stealing an interns car and speeding down Pennsylvania Ave as you answer the phone with hands not free. "Yeah, you got your president of the United States here. I'm driving so if this is important we can continue talking but I don't think I'll be able to survive if we talk." Yeah, see the Secret Service would be totally mind fucked at this moment. "Don't want me to do anything, did you forget the last time you told me no. That was about me using tooth paste off the self what do you think the fit that I'm going to throw the second you start in on 'I don't think a Russian spy would make an appropriate lover for the president of the United States?'" they whine no matter what. "you need to stop making custom chemicals for your bathing supplies" "I don't care that you have degrees in biology and chemistry" "It doesn't matter if it cleans better" "Stop adjusting the shampoo." "Who Fucking Nares a dog?"

There are solutions to everything that we are going through and I will break the Secret Service. They are no match for me. So Netflix is so hard up for movie Idea's how about this one I piss Trump off so much that he sues me. In the deposition where Trump tells me how I hurt his feelings, I use it to make a fool of the president. I mean make he explain in a coherent statement why me calling him a dumb ass hurts his feelings. Needing to do advanced crowed sourced multi attack factual verification network that pulls from the collective knowledge of the online community to gather all data pertinent to crushing Trump in court. I put the tape of the deposition on Amazon prime, Netflix, YouTube and everywhere else I can upload it in a caffeine fueled dissemination of Trump making a fool of himself. As each watch goes to fueling the lawsuit we would have constant news coverage of the movie for years.

There is a poetic balance that hatred spewed forth from a small man instead of hatred being created in the world but a silencing feedback loop forms drowning out the speaker in his own crap.

If he does good I'll be astonished even if it is accidental it would be a miracle. But I wouldn't deny the nose of my face. No matter how much I wouldn't want to see it. The same cannot be said for his voters. I'll say if you voted for Trump it was because of bigotry or that you have been taken in on stupid shit the Republicans have been saying for years. So you're a bad person or you are stupid. I don't see how they can be good Americas and have this stand. There is plenty of blame to go around those that voted for him even though it will make their life worse are an easy target. A party that has been saying for decades that smart people aren't the only ones that run a government and no one wonders why they have progressively been getting dumber with each generation. Where we have them constantly tormenting their constituents with promises never fulfilled and everything out of reach as those liberals are doing so much more than you and getting paid major dollars so they must be getting more welfare than you are. Welfare keeps you down and democrats are taking it all? I mean the nerve and not a single time would your mind go to hey Obama gave me one of the largest tax cuts of all time maybe my bad lot in life has more to do with the long term policies of where I grew up. Where the state governments are screwed up because of your vote.

Another power up and rocking to Icon for Hire I can pull through to the eight o'clock hour. I have clearly taken the power-up to early. But you got to make a move and my head is so thrown as my ears seem to be messing with themselves. Just shuffling random problems all contradictory. It's as almost as your body isn't suppose to take this kind of abuse or something. I'm sure you aren't thinking that even though I'm clearly pointing you in a direction that you should know that I'm having problems and have a slight need for a time ship. If you are so inclined, it would take not time at all and hardly a bother. Pick me up after you finish your errand or before, it is all relative. That call will now be put down in a written record for all time. I have the best chance of any person up until now to be visited by a time traveler. I say we set up the odds with a few categories. If I might have met someone that isn't from this time, did they seem like they weren't from this time, random guys that know about this stupid bet and want to fuck with us as they fake being time travelers. That is always the most traitorous part of time travel, fake travelers ruining a perfectly ordinary afternoon. Those kind of afternoons that you know something is up, just as two buffoons drop from the ceiling in gorilla suits. Moments before they jump into a four hour spiel about how they are going to save humanity with just my help. I do have especially stupid friends.

Close to the end your are like this isn't even entertaining anymore you've know this was fake for like going on fifteen minutes now and they have five minutes left in this entire thing. Should you just ignore them or walk away, what is the kind thing to do in that situation? I mean if they are true time travelers they would know that they would end up a failure the first time and would just pop up at another point in my life to prove that they can travel. How was that not obvious? Real time Travelers Knock, Twice.

Basics of time travel, don't think to hard about it. Bring a towel, turns out Douglas Adams had great insight when it comes to travel throughout the galaxy. The bible as it is known to people in the business as we adhere to those parts that will keep you alive when you leave the safe confines of our earthly sphere. It would be good to bring the entire six part spacey travels books. You can find them in paperback because you can never find a place to plug something in. Use the book and they will know that you are a traveler from earth and will take good care of you until you are ready to go home. Just don't do that one thing that Douglas Adams said to do because it was a joke. If you do that everyone will go nuts for like no reason what-so-ever. Other than that one thing the book it is perfect for space travel and time travel all over our universe. We that know His Bible believe that God was the first alien who travels from place to place improving the universe until we walk side by side with him. Those that carry His Bible believe as I do that Douglas Adams is the first alien.

He has been known to pass out knowledge of the truths of the universe in entertaining stories. He always is more awesome to those that know him. When it is between God and the Devil the first walks across battle fields bringing peace and unity where once there was discord the second brings sex, drugs and rock-n-roll just ask the crazy Jesus freaks of the late eighties. For those women who he loved all give a shutter and pass out when they think back on the time they got to spend with the pasty English man. I mean someone get me a picture to go on here. I'm pulling up nothing.

The media has a huge apology to the human race. For decades they have allowed republican to get away with lying on national television and still getting to come back on. This has set the stage for things that are wrong being taken as equal to those that are right. As Trump lied about everything for decades he should have just been banned from news since he couldn't tell the truth. I mean think of a world where everyone holds their honor as close to their vest as they do their life. If you get caught lying they won't have you go on national television ever again. Think of ending all chance of publicity as a news analysis got told a single lie out of your mouth. Then any argument that we have over reality could be litigated. I know it isn't perfect but it is better. We would have to set up a system to challenge pre-held notions. How about Philosophical Corners for philosophical questions? Where Physics are answered by physics professors instead of politicians. So science is reported rightly so everyone understands reality. We would have news that reports facts and draws from reality.

The thing is we couldn't make everyone abide by these standards. Not unless, we make the news person a professional calling. If you call yourself a News Person without the News Bar card is just as criminal as calling yourself a lawyer without passing the legal bar. News Persons must adhere to a certain standard or they go to jail like any inept doctor or incompetent lawyer. Okay, I can see where this goes off the rails and we might have to rethink this one. It wasn't a bad start and I'm thinking black listing would be a little much for a reporter being caught in a know lie but it would work. The ban on getting reported on if you are a known and proven liar. It wouldn't be looked down as much as being known as a Nazi but one day, maybe. It is not going to happen Nazi's are just in the wrong, always. Even without knowing the facts a good response to any situation that included Nazis is just to denounce everything that they stand for. I mean it doesn't matter if they were caught rescuing Jewish orphans from a fire that was set to frame them for a hate crime no one would attack you if you denounce the hatred their group spewed into the world.

Do you ever get that "I'm good but I don't say everything that crosses my mind." Where you feel guilty for doing this to your friends. You should also remember you need to measure yourself up against the proper morality stick. I know there are a lot of detestable people in the world today but do not be deluded to think that this is anything near normal. You must still use a proper stick, step one have you caught yourself not saying something because you seen someone that has different color skin than yours, you fail. The correct response was you caught yourself from saying something you know is inappropriate and you will try to be better next time. Remember you'll never be anything near perfect and you should punish yourself accordingly. But really make the punishment individualized so it sticks that you are not perfect. If you have kids you should start breaking down their self esteem now because they are ugly and the world is going to be so cruel to them.

Passing on what our family has used as punishment is an important tradition. With a look to inflicting truly specialized torture on children it brands there psychology to their lineage. This I believe ties the generations into the same job more that their inferior genes. More study will be needed to ensure that it is true. We will test for Family Induced Patheticness and Incompetence Contagion Disease. We will be able to stamp out those problems that we have in dealing with the very stupid. Some culture induced stupidity along with conditioned responses that makes the person self destructive choosing every crappy politician that crosses his path. I think that I have it figured out we got to cure democrats of being pussies. What more do we have to do, nothing. If we had one functional political party we wouldn't be at the current point would we. No, if democrats fought with the facts that republican states are welfare supported shitholes maybe those hicks would have seen the truth since it is more obvious than the nose of your face.

High Rant 20 Blood Thirsty Lawyers

    Here take the magical pipe. Don't worry as long as you breath in and provide fire the glass will yield a smooth high. It will sneak up on you with the quietest sounds that you have ever heard. Beating you to an inch of your sanity and then giving you an extra shove. It was built by the gods in Hel were the god of fire yields death, built with the choir of ripping the still beating hearts from the divine Pot Plants as she concentrates the hearts of these noble creatures into a pipe of the gods. Where this glass pipe is perfect for attuning with the universe itself. Yes glass, for all hearts are made of glass why do you think that they break so easily and why it is so precious when someone gives it to you.
    The quest to rip the hearts from the plants went heavy with mine but I promised to do anything they needed before finding out what I was in for. Bodies being stack fifty high I still had work to do. For these poor creatures is finding how cruel this universe is to such as these only because they are loved beyond their desire to break it off. How would we ever let this fine lady walk away but for only the briefest of moments. She'll be mine and I know just what to do put that shiny glass to your lips and feed the hole with holy fire and breath, as the life in the flames gives to enlightening holy mist. Or as the concentrate that we tried to smoke melted to the bottom and we have like an ounce of weed in concentrate to smoke hidden in the bottom of this pipe.
    My idea to let them use my pipe is looking like a highly brilliant plan. Who would possible keep attempting to smoke concentrate from a pipe until he stuffed half the tube into the bowl. It will be a while before the cleaning but that seems to be a little inconvenience when there is a month of good times awaiting us. I have lent my pipe to people before while I was using Sneaky Pete which required 2 bowls of weed to be able to smoke but one. One bowl wouldn't burn unless you knew it had to be turned over where the owner would always end up with a personal bowl to smoke himself. I call it a wear and tear fee.
    I mean use my wife but my weed and pipes that is where you are starting to get into an area where you need to resort to violence and now I can call the cops. I mean it always used to be a very barbaric process were we would use physical violence to solve who owns what but now we can involve lawyers. I mean, I love dog fights but to see lawyers rip each other apart gets my blood boiling. I love to toss in knifes that have electricity running throw the handle randomly. It is fighting and turrets. Man you starve a lawyer of clients for a few days and they are ready to go full Genghis Khan. I don't know what those Ivy Leagues do to the guys but they

turn into whinny little bitches. A few shots with a cattle prod and they are most agreeable. Granted it takes some time to teach them to fight but once you break their spirit they are ready to kill for you.

With legalization this will give us a greater shot at snagging some lawyers higher on the food chain. I heard about a legendary lawyer that didn't need any help in reaching feral form. He didn't need any training to break him down into the savage beast that he became. He takes drugs and sex in payment for pathetic defenses with intellectual support that has been described as the bare minimum required for adequate legal counsel. As with the increased calls from weed disputes in the home the opportunity that it has given us for an easier catch and train program is amazing. I prefer a weaning the chaff method. I snag lawyers in bulk and set them to destroying each other. I do lose some promising recruits that way. One that stood I kid you naught at a complete six foot four. It would make your heart break to hear what he weigh in at. Call me a traditionalist but these modern methods of training lawyers is just ruining the sport.

He was a great loss and a complete surprise as a first year law student went crazy. I mean, I have had sum berserkers but none that took to it so naturally. The big guy was a complete loss but we have all had a truly epic prospect that we had to put down because they just never got the blood thirsty drive. If only we could communicate with them but they don't seem to be able to get they have to advocate for their side until one dies. I mean you sick a lawyer on some person you better not see them again as long as that person's family and all distant relations are alive or you call them off but why would you do that. There is so many of them no one misses them when they disappear.

High Rant 21 The Science Mob

When it comes to the human race and evolution we have an interesting quandary that is brewing on our hands to talk about. We have survived for the last one hundred thousand years as human, an intellectual aware species, one who has beneficial traits that allowed us to become the dominate species on this planet. The traits are important, think if everything was the same but we were the size of the blue whale. This wouldn't be all that helpful as we would only have at a max population somewhere far south of a million. Any hope to be a space traveler is going to be totally shot for the entire species. Now if you go the other way as a species that possesses our current level of technology that was only big enough for their brains to comprehend this level of development. Any hope of advancing to a slip stream proportion drive for interstellar travel would be completely out. As the most their brains can comprehend is our current level, they would be forevermore stuck unless they start breading larger adults. Also the necessary computer development for intelligent computers to compensate for their small size doesn't develop without an intelligence that is far smarter that basic slip stream drives.

So we have a one hundred thousand year span of human history that we can clearly say we are able to draw a bright line where we have separated ourselves from other animals, a day where we started manipulating our environment on a global scale. Where everything that surrounds us is manufactured to manipulate what would have normally been there if there wasn't a constant evolution of social norms. Animals eventually lock in a certain set of behaviors after a few thousand years. The assumption of human survival is predicated that we as thinking beings will be able to outlive any normal mass extinction event that is coming. When we can look forward it sure seems bright. If that wasn't the case though and the higher ability to think and manipulate our environment will lead to a certain extinction we surely wouldn't be able to see it coming without further study.

When we look at some animals we see designs that have been the same for the last fifty or sixty million years. The designs are basic but the intelligence is different. So with a short time we must conclude that we don't have the information to determine if being a smart ass will get you killed off faster than being a dumb ass.

The argument for the existence of no intelligent life out there would also cut against those that wish to believe anything that you do matters. If the human race dies out nothing that we have will last long enough to be discovered by any alien species. So aliens don't exist because if they did we would have signals from them that they would have to be beaming out into space. They would also not be sending signals out if they were wiped out by their intelligence only a few hundred years after developing signals.

It would also be likely that there are species out there that are more intelligent than they would need to get them all killed but they live because they don't have the necessary equipment to use their intelligence to get them killed. Hence the blue whale that can't manipulate their environment. There are still plenty of species where their biology prevents them from any form of space travel. A simple electrical allergy for a species where they catch fire would certainly put them into a category that should be left out of whether it is more likely that an intelligent being will be wiped out of existence than a non intelligent one. If a species is unable to manipulate their environment to a level significant to be classified as an intelligent species they too should be eliminated, either intelligent enough or not.

Fairness would be all collective intellect species shouldn't be included in this study proposal due to they have never been classified as a species unless they have over four different minds. Any less than four different minds should be categorized as living relics and should be maintained as such. With the constant morphing of who's mind is where has never had a successful science study done. Feel free to check the primary literature.

So we should start this study on the most investigated species that we know about in our universe of knowledge. Human. They are a hardy species and firmly believe that they will be around forever. For the purposes of this study we will be looking at the question of average lifespan of the human species compared to those of comparable species of similar capabilities when it comes to survival in their environment. As this is a long term research project if we can raise all the money up front, than it will cost a fraction for continual month to month financing. We can conduct this study for one thousand dollars a year if we were to get the funding in full in advance. The closer we reach to the funding goal the cheaper that it will be in the long run. So the next one hundred million years at a thousand dollars a year we come to an upfront payment of one hundred billion.

With this assessment we hope to discover if the human race has a chance to survive in the future. We would hate to see something bad happen to your little species.

High Rant 22 Cheery Thoughts

Since we are on such cheery subjects like the destruction of the entire world due to a fundamental flaw in humanity we should ask the question. If the human species ends what worth would there have been to existence? It goes back to the question, if a tree falls in the forest and no one was there to see it, does it make a sound? Does the human species go down in the galactic ledgers as a zero if we blink out before anyone even knows we were here? Do alien species even like to look into the mysteries of the past? Would they show up the day after all humans died and just be interested if they can move in? No need to know about the ghosts in your rental property that have been left there from the broken hearts of those that came before you. Just a signature on a line and nothing about the souls of those others that were here too.

With the destruction of the human species before contact with extra terrestrials we can see that there is little hope for us to be registered as anything. Only the slim chance that an alien would stumble upon our planet due to the ending of radio signals that we have sent out or one of our ships that NASA has thrown out into the endless space screaming into the night that We...Are...Here! Than only a handful of relics would ever leave our world before everything has been wiped away.

What would they choice? Fine art or digital files to put together our last days. Would it be high science or a cheap thrill for those species that missed the cliff that humanity is screaming towards and think that they only just missed it. It could have been them as they scoff at a younger society because it is obvious that all the problems of their society have already been solved. Even if it was just random sex toys that they collect can you imagine what unlikely scenario that they would take anything of yours.

I mean what is the likely hood in even that most remote scenario that you would matter, even a little in the long run? When we look at it from anyway it doesn't seem like it would matter what I did. If you are so insignificant would it matter what I did to you. It would be like swatting a mosquito in Mississippi. No one would notice.

I rationalized it out, how about you fuck with me now.

High Rant 23 Science Proven Philosophical Goods

Is it a problem that getting high and bitching can be boring? What does it say that drug use and complaining no longer entertains constantly. I mean back in the old days we know that they turned their TVs off when there wasn't anything on them. It seems weird but they didn't have the over abundance that we have in TVs golden age. Even watching it on our phones all day long we aren't able to put a dent in everything that we want to see and it is only getting better have you seen Rick and Morty, high?

Now talking about how we should first watch a new show it does take some classification. Horror shows should be properly watched at night. There is nothing worse than watching a zombie eat someone's face as birds chirps outside. It takes a lot from the creepy vibe. So horrors, zombie, suspense are those that should be watched under the cover of night. Those guilty pleasures that you love to watch, at first look are to be put in the night watching category but there is different definitions of guilty and some are more disturbing than others. Porn should defiantly be watched where only those that have consented to watching it, can walk in on you. Those that you watch for the sex that isn't porn as in The L Word are best to be done under the cover of darkness. For those more perverted than that and would want to hide your enjoyment of something truly sick I would suggest using some kids to cover it up. It's fine if the little kids aren't paying attention as long as they are in the room while you are watching it no one would suspect that taking care of the kids is being used to cover up the sickest perversion. Early morning you'll find these people with their eyes glued to the TV watching My Pretty Pony. Horrible people, watching My Pretty Pony works best in the morning when you can pass off that loving affection in your eyes for sleepiness.

Since we are seeing that there is a good reason to alter how you watch something, might I put forward that Rick and Morty most appropriately, should be, watched when high during the first time. Now this isn't going down with the Half Baked, How High, Dazed and Confused and Forest Gump category but should go down for a completely different rational. Rick and Morty should go down for the adult comic category as being a reason for enhancement by gods little miracle.

God's little miracle that is a great name. I mean that is what we should call it from now on. Everyone needs to call it God's little miracle just think of the phrases that we would get. "They are trying to take away God's little miracle in the capital today in later news the abortion debate is back because of the politician having problems with God's little miracle." We would cut the opposition in half to legalizing across the entire United States. The only problems with it from there is the inevitable acceptance of our place in society. With so many in the population we deserve equal representation.

Every population complains about how little their representation is but look at this figure sixty percent of the population has smoked weed and we don't have a single openly smoking representative anywhere in the government. Yeah, those are the numbers. It makes the twenty percent of the population with no religion look petty by comparison when they ask for more representation. With sixty percent of the population we should be moved up in the cue to start getting some recognition for our contributions to society.

Making up a disproportional contribution to society while still be persecuted for providing what society has been enjoying and will continue to enjoy for decades to come. We gave you Dave Chappel and if you believe *Weed Madness,* Jazz. Can't we finally say that weed is accepted in our society. There isn't much that we need to do to adjust. Those of that use make up sixty percent of the population would like nothing to change but the persecution. When you come into my house and find my grow room, I would like you to keep your mouth shut. It will be the same after the persecution ends, just keep your mouth shut. I don't care if my shits the bomb or anything else that you want to tell me. I'll be deciding on how well my new strain is doing by how long you are left drooling in the dog food bowl.

There is a dichotomy to our species but there is also one that has been lost over the age between those that are both scientist and philosophers. Where small minded people years ago argued that science and philosophy should be separated because even smaller minded people tried to integrate god into science with philosophy. Philosophy and science are both seeking truth but from different angles. Science tells me how much THC is in God's little miracle and philosophy tells me that it is good. Science and philosophy doesn't always agree but because they do we should just accept God's little miracle.

Why do we back down from the small minded even if you insult them they won't understand. Pointing out that any inclusion of science into philosophical inquiry must remain science and not saying god exits. Instead of pointing out that they have failed at the science part we separated science and philosophy. How about we use science to determine what causes the greatest good in the world and call them Science Proven Philosophical Goods? It wouldn't take much to figure out just a few electrodes and a massive research project and we would be good to go. Philosophy in a utilitarian system is concerned with what is the best high and that is someplace that I think that science and philosophy can come together to solve.

High Rant 24 The Good Kind of Racism

The second the good kind of racism comes out of my mouth I seem to be in trouble with those around me. I mean you can love the French because they are French but because they are slutty and people start complaining. All they want to do is smoke cigarettes and have sex. We have a military they hire other people to fight for them so they can smoke cigarettes and have sex. I don't see that as a problem when looking at them or their society, I see it as a reason to go to France.

It is only the problem when bad stereotypes contaminate bigotry. That does sound weird. What if people only believed the good stereotypes? Is it justifiable if that was the case? You can hear some of the conversations if only good stereotypes were uttered "Man, I wish I had some cool stereotypes, like good at sports all I got is money and am allowed to get away with anything." "You should feel lucky all I got is I'm ruling the world behind the scenes." One would imagine those that are ruling the world would have to shift to persons unknown when the world is on the wrong tract. "It is a shame that they lost control of the world. I hope they get it back soon." Even that seems like a lot of work.

I have an easy solution to these problems, I only care about them in how they affect me. Caring about others have gotten us into this situation in the first place. It takes a lot of effort to care about someone that you have never met. I'm much too lazy to spend that much effort on anyone. I don't spend that much energy on people that I want to have sex with. Why would you spend so much energy and get nothing back? Just ignore it unless it affects your life. When a cop shoots someone in the back don't get upset about the guy dying that has nothing to do with you. Getting upset in that situation should be about how you will no longer will be able to get news because it will be 24/7 breaking news coverage of the shooting. You could also get upset about the complete refusal to put in reforms that could stop it from every happening again.

How the news reports things is something that you should get upset about. I mean out of the twelve hundred people that are shot a year by the police how can it possible be breaking news. We have three people every day in the United States that get shot by cops, every day all year long. How can any off this be anything else than just a manufactured artificial sense of irregularity to pump the ratings? With cop deaths sitting at under two hundred a year wouldn't it seem more realistic if they did that for cops. Even though half of the deaths in the line of duty happen due to prolong doughnut consumption. That might seem mean unless you think someone that can fire sixteen bullets into a child's back then lie about it, have his fellow officers to lie for him, have internal affairs cover it up even when there is a video and then be immune to prosecution for years. After, all that we also should prevent anyone in make fun of the officer because they should also be immune to our only remedy.

With breaking news happening on a daily basis should it really be a surprise. There is a graph out there waiting to be brought forth from the void. One that will have a regressive line that slices through an oscillating line that reveals how long from the last breaking news will the media use the breaking news again determined on how large the news that they can drum up is. Given particularly long dry spells they will start taking anything so they can...scratch...that...itch. "Breaking News We Have A Squirrel That Is Riding Little Skies." Granted that would be after a month of no cop shootings though.

With how much that they are invested in by the people of this still free country I say we ask for some professionalism. We make lawyers pass a bar to eliminate the worst of them. Yeah, it was painful to admit that the lawyers that we have now are better than the lawyers that we would have without the bar. So we have professional journalist and only they can produce news. We take it back to where we don't have to deal with people coming out on the news and lying to us all the time. If you lie you have to make up for the lie before you get to get back on the news. It sounds simple but if you call yourself the news how can you constantly report the words of a known liar.

Think of the politicians. You want to get elected than you have to go on TV and to stay on TV you can't lie. I think, I converted the majority of those that read the opening sentence of this paragraph. If you didn't read the first sentence of this paragraph are you trying something new? It seems like that would be a very weird thing to do. So all we need to do is get this argument into the hands of every reader so we can finally get professional journalists. Yeah, free publicity.

I mean we would have to put some other restrictions to improve the process a little. First, I would teach them not to allow roughing of the refs. You have news coverage of an idiot that it saying that the news won't cover him and the people in the news rooms are thinking 'I'll show him, it doesn't matter if he has Been Wrong For THe LAst TWEnty YEARs WE'LL CARRY HIS ENTIRE SPEECH LIVE'. People say the media is biased against them and man you can't find a journalist that will ask that man a serious question, anywhere.

Well those are my idea's for a journalism over-hall and maybe a Science Review Board. It's simple if you have a question about science you bring it to the Science Review Board and they will tell you global warming is happening and that the industry lawyer isn't someone you should listen to about weather. It wouldn't be that hard to stop reporting fake things and lies we just have to decide that we will make them admit the truth.

Ben Lemon

High Rant 25 Erasing History

The question is what do we owe the generations that came before? I will give you, before we even ask that question, I'll accept anything you want to give those that are still alive as a reward or a thank you for having sex. I don't see any problem with that but I'm asking about do we owe them in keeping the human race going? We could easily now develop permanent birth control for the world while ending the birth of new people we could start putting research dollars into producing an even higher end of life care every year. In twenty years we wouldn't have to spend anything on kindergartens, elementary, junior and high schools.

Producing robots that will take the place of the aging nursing staff. With the advancements we've seen already I'm sure by the time we get to the last people they'll have robots that can tend to their every need. They'll be advancements in medications that is a sure thing. Medication to give a permanent level six high while taking care to exercise your body as you lay around. Nothing to do but watch as the walls of you home start to take on a life of their own. Crazy characters are fighting, throwing benches and chairs over who is to pay for lunch as the fight takes on a life of its own as neighbors take to the street in unending rows of homes that empty one by one. As we slide away from the humanity to watch from above as the buildings start taking sides. Moving to one side of town and back again as ground is gained and lost a thousand times. With the governor worried of course as the one thing he can manage to do is make the problem worse.

Cops, deputies and a dog that dreamed one day of being the thin blue line that kept squirrels away from the house. It isn't that squirrels are all bad it is just funny when they die. I mean think of any squirrel death and not get a smile on your face. A squirrel's head stuck in an oven, A squirrel hanging himself, walking in on your wife and another squirrel so you kill them both with a shotgun and two responding squirrel officers before turning the gun and blowing squirrel brains all over the ceiling. Are any one of those not just completely hilarious? That isn't the only reasons to keep them away from the house, they just seem shifty. All that chattering back and forth they are clearly up to no good. How much can you possible talk to one person who isn't master? Then there is their complete disregard for authority.

Do you know how many time squirrels threw a party on my roof in the middle of the night? They are clearly setting up alibis to do some nefarious things. My master must be protected for he is too gullible and kind for he thinks that squirrels shouldn't be all treated to the sweet cold kiss of death. Why should we allow them to suffer life? They are clearly deranged and need to be put down for their own benefit.

High Rants

So in a little over a hundred and fifty years from now this Earth could be depleted of humans. There wouldn't be a fuse. All people would see would be the embers slowly dying as the population shot towards zero.

So what do we owe those that came before? Everything they did would disappear with the last death. We know it isn't likely that any species would ever find our civilization before it is eaten away by time. Every generation carries a larger portion of a burden than the one before. As we move forward there will always be more to carry.

If completely wiping out the human race is too much than how about just deleting a piece of the human soul. The complete eraser of a major and significant event throughout all records and memory. How about we decide to eliminate something that we don't want in our past to make us feel better about what happened, just erasing a blight on the human soul. Eliminating Pearl Harbor as the blight that it is on the United States as it was the reason to get into WW2 instead of Hitler being a total dick and Japan doesn't like the sneak attack that it has become to be known as. An effort to rewrite real events to a plausible cover story and then the complete scrubbing of any written or video account that says otherwise and then just decades of pretend before there isn't anyone alive that remembers what really happened.

High Rant 26 Grumpy Bitch

    Look man. I tell you don't do it. That bitch if fucking crazy. On top of all that she is constantly grumpy as in, all the time, for no reason whatsoever. Her entire life is sitting on her ass and eating what could possibly be the thing that is making her that irritated. In all seriousness she tried to bit the throat out of the last one. I mean, I'm into some kinky shit but I don't want to have to protect my throat while I'm keeping it in. That seems like a little too much work for some tail.
    Why isn't this talking you out of it?
    Have you heard a single word I said?
    I mean, you must be hard up to hit that. You will go after things that I wouldn't touch in a million years of celibacy. That poodle is a total cunt but if you need to. She'll only break your heart.

High Rant 27 Protocoligorically Correct

When you are stuck, start with the first rule, it's a fine rule, that is why it is the first rule. It has been around since the beginning. Surely it will end up being the last rule, even when it always remains the first rule. If the rule always comes first than it must be the most important rule and as such the most important rule should come first, to avoid any confusion about what the most import one is. But, to be protocoligorically correct, the rules should be written down so we can reference the rules and in what order we find them, so to, in what order the arrangement of the rules can be determined as you leave out the first rule. Now the first rule, being first, it should be seen as everyone understand it to be first and writing it down would just be redundant. As the first rule, is first and clearly everybody knows the rule, you should never even bother to write it down. That shouldn't even be an issue since none of us need to learn the first rule, since it's never written because obviously we all already know it. Since the first rule isn't written down it shouldn't be counted and added to the total amount of the rules to follow. So, we all know that when we read a list of rules, we should start with two which is the rule that we label one which isn't the first. So a list of ten rules should always be read from rule 2 to rule 11 listed as #1-10. This does simplify rules. Now that they are written down in a protocoligorically correct fashion the first rule isn't there as you already know it. As writing down the first rule would become redundant as to the understanding that we all know the first rule for any list of rules we must follow.

High Rant 28 White Woman's Privilege

I always feel that I don't get the necessary respect when it comes to dealing with my girlfriends parents in any upcoming meeting. Sure there have been times where say I asked her mother to join us, you know, in naked fun time, I mean sex. I asked a mom for a threesome with her daughter. This has happened but in my defense after the request was made she still ended up with one of my chainmailie bras. Long after me and her daughter hit it and quit I still involved myself in their life, for years. Now If I still can be friends with the "Threesome Mom" don't you think that I can handle your parents.

Back in high school I was called Eddie by my girlfriend's mom. Like the in *Leave it to Beaver* the one kid that can't do anything wrong. Every time he opens his mouth he has the absolute right thing to say in the moment brown noising the parents is required so they never believe anything bad the kid is accused of. "Eddie, I love Eddie" "What do you mean Eddie was caught with my daughter, he's such a good boy he would never do that." "Clearly sex trafficking is bad but any part that Eddie had must have been quince-dental." And you call these people kiss asses, TO SHAME THEM. I mean a few right words to get whatever you want, Hmmm, let me think on this. How can any *kiss ass* even care about you people that live on a lesser plane on human morality I say?

I do say that *kiss asses* are morality better than you all. Back when I was being ashamed for being a *kiss ass* my girlfriend and her mother started to get into it. I was standing there with the answer. For the warm-up it looked like it was going to be a blazing fire in mere moments. I leaned in to my girlfriends ear and whispered my answer and I could see a roaring blaze coming my way. There is one thing that you never do when dating a white woman's daughter and that is to get into the middle of a fight between her daughter and her. We know this and I bravely stepped in, if the response that I calculated was even a fraction off you know that white woman privilege was going to kick in. White woman privilege she expects to be allowed to do anything she wants and not get arrested. All she would need is one woman show up in a uniform that is either a mother, a daughter or a man that looks at the situation and says "Fuck the law. I'm not getting involved with this." who will then clearly see that that nasty thing with the fishing pole, was clearly called for. Or a husband that has a daughter (Need to Clarify who I'm have a problem with or you might oppress the wrong people, because obviously you are too stupid to make up your own mind and are letting Hollywood use you as a puppet.) because he knows how crazy his wife would get in the same spot and go "Well she did stop after half an hour, does seem like she was being reasonable." or any man that has ever dealt with a crazy woman and as my girlfriend uttered my words a cool breeze blasted away the anger in her mother's face. The force of the cooling even disrupted the leaves of the fall that was laying on the ground around her. Blasting out from the epicenter. Nature herself was like "Aah, that was perfect."

Anyone that seen that would say that my feat was that of such epicness that I would never be forgotten. Now throwing down for an epic feat to save the world from pain is morally better than protecting yourself. Even the act of making someone happy by smiling and telling them that they are beautiful makes the world a better place and I am clearly a Utilitarianism and a Kantian good. This maxim is easy to accept for anyone.

So I call out to all *kiss asses* of the world to stand up proud. Those that hate us, would have us stop spreading the joy we bring to the world. Are we going to allow that? We could stop but that only means that those that want the world to be miserable would win. So when they are making fun of you, go to them. Tell them that their jaded barbs hurt so bad that you're going to need therapy. The painful and hurtful jokes has completely broken your spirit and will to live. Never have you been hurt so badly. They are some of the greatest people in the world when it comes to inflicting pain.

Yielding to the pain you let out a tear as the compassion of the nearest girl causes her to come and make you feel better. Causing you to admit that no one has comforted you more in your entire life. Having her throw her body as a band-aid over the damaged pieces of your soul. The pain of your soul just feels like it has softened since she is there and you can imagine a day with her when she will have scrubbed every bit of your pain that you have lived with for years, away.

There is no need to tell her you already have a girl because that wouldn't be in the higher morality of the *kiss ass* leaving everyone you meet feeling better than they should in all rightly-hood have the right to. I mean have you seen some of the morons out there. In your mind think of the average girl out there and assign her to the proper level of stupidity, now you know that half of the population is even dumber than that. So obviously your girlfriend doesn't need to know because statistically she has a fifty percent chance in being in the stupid half. I haven't found a proper way to explain why my dick was seen cheating on my girlfriend and I shouldn't be blamed as an extension to my penis or why my penis shouldn't be blamed or most importantly, harmed for its action. I also shouldn't be expected to explain it to a girl satisfactorily that only has a fifty-fifty shot of being above average and smart enough to get it. If I lucked out and got to date a beautiful and smart girl she would defiantly understand how kindness to me should be rewarded.

High Rant 29 Philosophy and Star Trek

My philosophy is one that I've developed on my own as a child. I had some influence from Buckminster Fuller's book Critical Path in the ninth grade but before that, it was an instinctual level understanding of philosophy built upon with reason and reflection. Something that was completely new, especially to me because I grew up in an absence of excessive intellectual conversations. Building in up over the years, when I worked out new final grounding for anything I gather another set of building blocks to rise even higher than before. I called this Reductionalism, before I found a philosophy that was called Reductionism. It is a shame that any generation had to grow up without the ability in accessing all the knowledge in the world. We are indeed leaving our children a better world. I've taken to calling it Minimalism for want of a better name. I should try and figure out a better one before I'm stuck with Minimalism that will forever share it's name with a nineteen fifty's architecture movement. Even though it is similar in thought, I'm afraid to link the two as it may cause some confusion in lesser minds.

So the hunt for a better name should be taken before this book is published. As I have already said some horrendous things in 1-28 I would imagine that the lawyers would not let me release this. Creating a situation where I know that I should finally pick a name to go with my philosophy since I've been working on it for decades but the fact that if no one finds out about the specifics of my philosophy it won't matter how many times I change the name or how long it takes to settle on one. That being said I should look to use this topic to make my book longer, just to make more money off of you.

Naming a system of thinking should be reflective on what the system is so it is easy to place it when you are learning about philosophy. Which today is one of the biggest parts of philosophy. Utilitarianism is one that I use a lot since its name reflects its underlining logic. I know that it has been lost over time but Utilitarianism was the grade A perfect name to a way of thinking on par with the high five in name perfection. Today it would be named something to the extent of Hell Ya, Lets Make Everyone Feel Good. Now you see why it appeals to me so that should be kept in mind.

With that being said you should first understand my philosophy as a Unifying Theorem, A Great White Wale Wall Mount, Epic Awesomeness, a Key to Deeper Understanding. It isn't needed to stick in a single philosophy it works in every philosophy that anyone has thought up. It's the Universal Decoder to the Universe and your entire life. So we will need a name on balance with that. See my problem?

High Rants

It doesn't start from a question as "Would you turn a train killing one person or letting it continue on its path killing five?" There is the basic problem with the question in the first place. First we need to define the Moral problem of death. Understanding where it begins and what we are using as a basic building block, we then determine why are actions in themselves good or ill. This is fundamental to have a coherent and consistent philosophy. Which I know everyone desires above all else, it isn't like people would manipulate what their philosophy is for their own benefit, is it?

So if we look at the future of the human race as inevitable like a river; any stone thrown into it disappears into the destiny of the river no matter what you try the future of the human race is set in stone forever waiting for us. This does set some interesting things in motion. With a destiny to meet us any death is insignificant so the question isn't would you kill one or let five die, the question is "Would you be doing anything?"

For any deterministic look Minimalism would bring us to the conclusion that we are immune from any moral blame for any action ever taken. Like a computer isn't blamed for all the Nazi's that end up with head shots in a game. So we have a need for a universe that our actions determine the future and where the future isn't set in stone or in simple terms a universe that doesn't need a time machine for free will to take place. (The Murdoch Hypothesis) With a universe where our actions can be justified as morally praiseworthy we can start making some progress with the questions to the question.

Being able to say something is morally praiseworthy is the goal of philosophy but it needs a basis for the statement and that is what my philosophy Minimalism is. It is the legs that hold up all things in philosophy. Taking things down to what the belief is based on. Why should we value life? This is the first question we must answer. This isn't an absolute right in any culture or country of the world, never has been. There is plenty of killings, executions, war, neglect and health care deficiencies needed to be taken care of before you get mad at me for the question if someone dies "Is it a bad thing?" The priorities should lay with preventing death then getting pissy with someone for asking philosophical questions.

Those most homophobic people are great as they are the easiest to get a blow job from. You just have to pretend that they are too drunk for them to be responsible for their actions or that it isn't gay because you don't know his name and it isn't going to be an ongoing thing or the like. I mean if they aren't gay what is the argument "being gay is 'easier' than being straight" all about. I want everyone to pretend that homophobic people are too drunk to be responsible for their actions. It is because we know that they are gay but they only feel comfortable being themselves when they think they aren't responsible for their actions. We should be kind to these poor, pathetic people. Think of how hard life has been for them, for them to think that other people are just handed everything. In a world where they can't make it because they aren't good enough they see others that have and just bitch. So we should be kind to them and pretend that they are drunk, too drunk to be responsible for the blow job they currently giving me.

Lawrence: My lines have been written for me in advance. I've never had to do this for an introduction but they are there so I can use them. Welcome my next guest who is on the New York Times Best Sellers list the writer of High Rants Ben Lemon.
Ben: Thanks for having me. I want to say that I didn't prepare in advance, which is to say that I didn't study but I am high, so that's a plus.
The difference in my intellect Normal and Enhanced is the difference of an entire plan laid out and a leap of faith that my superior intellect will catch me on the way down. And, yes I'm high and still have a superior intellect so obviously I have a healthy ego. Healthy like you hear an "Oh, my god you ran over my leg!" and you know that you couldn't possibly be responsible for that, so you just go, as to not complicate the matter anymore.

Travel into the TV is something that I have wanted to do forever. Hopping into the Star Trek universe would be awesome except for the obscenely high mortality rate of the species in such a fashion that there won't be any more humans left after twenty years. The good news is that they'll have an anomaly at any moment that will create the federation out of whole cloth so the story can continue. With voyager the first order of business is to see the doctor and get the augment upgrade. It has been decades since professor Soong worked on improving the human genome so there must be amazing advances that the Doctor can give you and it isn't tough to convince him to do something stupid. I mean Bashir had the most basic package and he wasted it away on pretending to be normal. Why not a reclusive genius designing everything for the federation and shunning everyone but a few women? This would seem to be the right way to go about it. With the Federation getting upgraded equipment every few years they all seem stupid enough not to look a gift horse in the mouth. No one would come looking to poke holes in the golden goose.
If you don't believe me look back at the first episode of Enterprise where they entirely miss signs that something is completely fucked. Act like nothing is going on. Being barley are able to avoid killing an intelligent being. With their superior morals they forgive the guy that was trying to scam them with an alien that he captured, tortured, starved and forced into slavery. I mean, if you are sorry that you did something you should totally be forgiven after you are caught and apologize, we'll gladly do the work you were suppose to in the first place.

High Rants

The universe of Star Trek is perfectly fine with me becoming an augment. Voyager would be good as I would have use of all the systems to prove that I'm better than everyone there. I won't need to become an augment to prove that I'm better than everyone it would just give them an excuse for why that can never beat me. I'm always trying to give people excuses for their sorry performance but sometimes they just don't see the freebie. It is probably because they are stupid. I shouldn't blame them much for that.

If you look at the universe there does seem to be glaring places where they are overlooking opportunities. Holodecks seem to be an endless free labor source. We have seen in Voyager that you can project holograms over a sizable portion of a planet with hardly any power usage. I mean just think of that. Building a city in a few weeks and all the people have to do is advance the holographic grid. There isn't even a need for human like workers. Why would you use an old doctor copy to mine? You can amp up the amount of strength a hologram has up to a few thousand pounds per square inch at least so the doctor copies struggling to get a rock into a wheelbarrow is just dumb.

Taking of the stupidity of using Doctors to mine in that fashion we have to look at the bigger picture. If they have Doctors then the entire thing is surrounded by holographic systems. This gives us the ability to make simple digging robots with a jackhammer for a chest piece, four arms and the ability to float over the ground. Along with this mindless automaton a conveyor belt that runs down every tunnel dragging all the rocks mined to the surface. It would only have to be a one way conveyor belt magically appearing from a wall.

DS9 wouldn't be so bad if it is in the first few years as you could blackmail Bashir to augment you out. Hey, after it's done you should know that augments don't like you normals judging us. How we relate to each other in the hidden augment community is our concern. You don't get to judge a community that has to hide what an ethically questionable medical procedure turn us into. There is no way you can understand our struggles. I thought bigotry was outlawed by this time or does my superior strength need to meet that week face of yours.

I would immediately start working on immortality. I'm not talking about downloading your mind into a computer. I'm talking about the full enchilada. Eternal youth and vitality. The holy grail of the immortality community. Even the vampires envy those with the platinum card to the end of the universe.

Starting, I would go full sleeper. Yes, that is right I would encase myself in a full sleeper pod for interstellar travel they used before warp drives. Giving me tens of thousands of years to solve immortality. Connecting holographic emitters and a computer to keep my mind active while I'm in long term storage I'll be able to interact with the outside world. Building a lab that far outstrips all others I'll move in a single path to discovering the key to eternal youth and vitality. Never again would you have to fear growing old or find time to take care of your bathroom routine. I mean giving up on sex for a few thousand years is hard but having someone whip your genetic code into something that is to be feared and extremely useful would make up for it.

    Not to mention that I would be the smarted person there. Even the Qs seem beyond all hope for logic and correct answers.

High Rant 30 Back Blurb

Come and get it. There is no need to wait with this book you'll get Moral Deserts. For philosophy has never been this fun as you get to ponder the questions of the universe like you were doing it high. You'll go through the ups and downs of a drug induced euphoric bliss. It has never been this chill in philosophy since the hippies.

Wow, look at that, I have solved the drug problems of the world. It took all this time but we now know how to do it. I have eliminated all the bad effects of experiencing God's little miracle that sweet Mary Jane. Now you'll be able to say that you have had multiple experiences and you just don't need any right now. Why would you, you are reading my book? No longer will you have that dazed head that always last not long enough or having to do anything to your body that would damage it. You can sit back and enjoy a completely clean, safe and fun experience with Mary Jane.

With this solution to ending drug use across this nation will also need each and every one whose eyes have read this to start peddling it. I mean, get it into the hands of everyone in your life. Give them the first one for free, just to see if they like it. If you can stop your family from doing drugs don't you think that it is the right thing to do. As this plan rolls out, I'll take on the responsibility to continue to get high so people everywhere will be free of this scourge.

I know, I can't believe he used part of a chapter for the blurb at the back of the book. I mean he wasn't planning it that way. Kind of like when a beautiful blond just falls into to your lap at a party. You don't have to use her but it just seems like you should.

Bravery, my name is Ben. I will bear the burden of the human race and go on to get high and write so everyone far and wide can sit down and relax into a perfectly harmless bliss of Mary Jane's torment. I don't ask for much just the millions that I will get from book sales as you send me damaged girl after damaged girl to "assist me."

Yes, it may seem bad that I'm after damaged girls but look at it from my point. They put out, they don't know they deserve better and just a little love and you can convince them to do anything for you. I got bored of this blond a few years back so I've told her if she loved me she should go with me to Paris but it doesn't look like we are able to afford being booked on the same flight. So she took the early flight as I pack up my stuff and moved back to Washington.

So people complain about how I treat woman. Throwing around suggestions that I should treat people better, like I want to be treated. If people let me be me as I get away with whatever I want, why should I curb my behavior? There seems to be a disconnect when it comes to who you should be talking to. Asking a wolf to stop eating all the chickens in the house is just as useless as trying to stop me from having whatever I want with the girls that get in my orbit, whenever I want it.

Feminism it is a unique word. You can give your long definitions but what it is Your not an Asshole to Women; second definition men and woman are equal. It is a very polite way of say "Hi, my name is Ben and I'm not a very specific type of asshole to woman." It is a very specific type of asshole. Yes, that is a lot to say when you first meet someone so they came up with a very specific word. I think that it would scare most off if you used the definition. It is in the subset of words that are only to be used in special circumstances of needing to obscure what you are really saying.

Now a Succubus is something that has an unnecessary word. I mean a Succubus is a female demon that has the power to get men to do her biding until their entire life is in ruins where all they have left is to embrace the sweet kiss of death. So, we are talking your typical female. I don't want to over categorize everything but when has a relationship ended any other way. Those that say they ended peacefully are only half of the couple as the other one repeats the same phrase as well gritting their teeth hoping to jump out a window.

Women have been using men's stupidity against them for thousands of years. It is one of the constants about girls which isn't saying much but since it can be relied upon we shouldn't over look one gift of sorts in the mouth. Controlling a woman has always been impossible. The second your pecker is in her hand she will have the key to the chains and you know for sure that it was your "idea." Think it goes all the way back to Adam and Eve when she brought him a few slices of fruit. That wasn't a simple story it was a fable, it was a warning written for all times to come. Women are dangerous not even god can control one.

"Here my children, this is all for you to rule over. Eat from the gardens, drink from the river, you and your decedents will live here forever. Just, don't eat from this one tree. Don't touch. Best if you just don't go near it. Forget about the tree except in the way that you remember that you shouldn't eat anything from this tree. Please whatever you do don't eat this fruit." Half a day later. "What have you done I told you not to eat from this tree." So he sent them out to live out their lives with pain and evil. "So look alright, the first two that fuck this up was Adam and Eve. They didn't listen to me so let me make this clear you eat fruit from this tree you will condemn yourself to suffering, pain and misery until you die of what could be a very painful death."

I wonder how many times god set up that experiment before giving up. And people complain about how much I point out the many incestual parts of the bible as proof of my hatred of god. See I go out of my way to cover up for Adam and Eve's obviously having incestuous kids. Like the immorality of eating of the fruit increased the evil in their hearts to such an extent that Cain killed Abel. That would explain why we are better than we have ever been before. Years of evil draining from humanity with each death as the evil is divided with each child. Or it could be the large swath of the country that gave up religion and joined rational people in committing less crime. There isn't a magical savior that will forgive your crimes so wasting time in prison, just wastes time you could be having sex and doing drugs. Okay, willing sex. There are so many sins to partake in why would you waist any of your time thinking about religious people. You know the percentage of Christians in prison? How about Atheists? "Stop Slaying, Savior Sin" and you wonder why is was the snake sound is spelled...ssss.

The biggest problem with this entire situation is we can clearly see that God is a girl. Let us look at the facts. Eve brought Adam the food to eat. It is instinctual for a man to eat food fetched by a woman. Two, men do what women want, to get sex, should we be held up every time we brake a few laws to get into a woman's pants? This does seem like clear evidence that God doesn't quite understand what it is like to be a man. If you were the second people to get down to Earth would you admit you made the same mistake or would you blame Adam and Eve for God making you to avoid the obvious incest? This would end one of the many incestual stories of the Bible.

Now, there is a creature that has power over all women. This mythical creature has one of the most powerful abilities of all, an Incubus. An Incubus, has the ability to control the actions of women and that is why I nominate the Incubus as the official mascot of the man. We hail the first kings of men and the last Incubus' everywhere. More powerful than god at least in the way it counts.

Now since you understand that anything that I've done to my ex's has been their wish. I don't see how you can see it any other way.

High Rant 31 Scientific Research

So, this one is important I have interrupted one of the most enjoyable chill sessions on no record. This is an important one so you should think of this for what it is. When you read back what I wrote, you know that it is the way it goes, when your high but you don't remember it like this. My memories of getting high are nothing like the high that you've read. If the transcendence that we achieve can't properly be remembered by the sleeping mind, than how do we know what it is like for mushrooms and LSD? We have watched them be taken and they can tell us what they've remember afterwards because they aren't remembering properly. The difference between what I remember and what I wrote is staggering.

This is the question? What do we really understand about (   ) and what do they really do? We can clearly see that the high isn't anything like what we can remember. Inducing an even greater extent to the mental manipulation can't have an improvement in memory retention. In looking at these flaws we can clearly see that those that have been doing work in addiction have been falling down on their jobs. We shouldn't be needing to be studying these things now, but this lack of knowledge must be correct immediately. I propose a clearly scientific way to see what is going on while under the influence.

We start off with modern dance, this is a must. For the ability to throw yourself around to such an extent that it looks a little creepy doing it anywhere but on a stage will be necessary. Then there would be the extensive build up of vocabulary to get the full range of ways to explain what is going on. There will be a need for practice so I will have to continue to write these rants if nothing else threatening to release six times the amount of books of High Rants that I have released previously before you even can make it to the courthouse and file an injunction against them and try to figure out how many times that your client has been brought up. I mean, if I have embarrassed him in anyway and he can get it up for a lawsuit I will guarantee that I'm going to be pissed off even more if you don't try to stop me from releasing my next six fold increase in books of High Rants.

That would be necessary because I believe that there are people out there that might stop our wondrous scientific endeavor and would do anything to stop us. Plus the dance moves would really help me out to avoid anything that will jump out at me during our research. I mean, I know that they won't be real but they could use computer graphics and put them in latter. The researchers could see what is going on and the public might get a peek into the important work that is being done. I for see a franchise High Life that will follow my graceful moves throw a world of computer animation. You thought that the dance was just for science no reason science shouldn't make me bank. I mean they are responsible for every dime everyone else has why shouldn't they have a little. Yeah, science made everything you own possible.

O my god, you have an antique end table from the 1700s ah how cute. Without science you didn't have the ability for this level of stability that we have had for the last three hundred years. So if we didn't have science your end table would have been rotted throw or used as a barricade against the pillagers. Yeah, science made everything you own possible.

High Rant 32 Back Woods Preacher

Mythology is a unique subject when looking at anything you have to know what peaces make it up. Some from the bible, then there is the D&D component, movies that reference or show them, folk lore and all too often it is the town preacher that messes up on his demonology. I mean come on what use is a preacher that isn't up to date on his demonology. I mean we take a demon that doesn't fly and just because some back water preacher tells the towns people the wrong name of the demon that carried off the little girl we have another demon with wings. I know the thought that we make up our own reality really kicks in here doesn't it.

With the notion that we believe things into existence does cause some major problems when we can't keep the demonology straight. Would it really be all that tough just to work out the demonology once and for all. We already touched on the demon class of Succubus/Incubus and looking back there is more to say. It is always easy to find something that you left out of mythical creatures since they don't exist. But for a Succubus we know that they started with the pissed off first wives.

It isn't hard to see why women obviously demonize the girls that catches their husbands eyes. This is a normal cattiness we find all too often. Now days they are just called sluts and that is all to be done about it, but back in the day women were to remain untouched so obviously the easy solution was to make them demons. Now the horns would come from being a demon that goes back to when Pan was turned in to a personification of the devil. I mean the catholic church hasn't used many tools to get rid of the pagans but making their god our devil did work really well, much better than the murders. The wings come from the angel that was the father to all the Succubus/Incubus.

High Rant 33 Bringing the Stabby, Stab, Stab

What would you do with forever? Would it be just watching the world turn? Molding humanity throughout the ages? What would it look like? Immortality is one of the most desired wishes right after the perfect health of your early twenties. I mean immortality is great but once you figure out that being immortal doesn't automatically give you a healthy body and eternal youth makes it two wishes.

The trick about wishes it is in the phrasing. I wouldn't like to call all genies cheep because that would be bigoted. It should just be said that as a fountain of wishes maybe they should try a little harder to fulfill the intent of the wish. When you say that you would like a large cock it would be nice if they didn't pretend that you meant that you would like a FUCKING ROSTER. I mean what would you like more a giant roster or a large cock? For those of you that just got pissed at me for denigrating raising chicken, FUCK YOU. The only way you can even possibly believe that crap is if you are being intentionally stupid.

The most problematic part of making a wish is the most useful part of curses. The obvious loop holes in making a wish, something you don't want can also translate into how you can get out of curses. "Don't throw me in the brier bush." If you can't write the loop hole yourself with tricking the curse-er with some nicely placed words than your only hope is getting your hands on the wording of the curse. I would suggest asking an oracle or a soothsayer and if you used up your questions there already than you have better been living and extraordinarily life. Questions to oracles must be saved for real need not thrown away on trivial things.

So saying you used up your questions on the local soothsayer or oracle I would say that your best bet is to find another that is willing to answer your questions. If you can't find another one you can always snoop, often you'll find that it is written down in a diary or stuck in a suitcase of your stuff as her last thought before shutting that chapter on her life.

When you get the exact wordings of the curse this part is critical, you must determine what kind of curse was put on you. Can you get it removed by making up with your ex. Sometimes just sending flowers can get you out off some of the toughest situations. If that isn't going to help or maybe she is not worth taking another moment of your time. I know a guy that has lived celibate for over a thousand years because he was cursed with instant death the next time he has sex. Yeah, I know he showed that bitch.

After deciding what type of curse it is you can further narrow down your solutions. Local folklore can come in helpful maybe there is a fairy pond that is all purifying or a fountain that sprung up from the tears of a saint. At this point in your search I wouldn't over look anything or any thread of information leading you on your quest.

So we have the Auto Breakers, the Loopholes and Questing when it comes to the Questing category we are divided into two different actions. We can either learn a lesson from the curse there by becoming a better person where we would never again commit the sin that put us here or go on a potentially life threatening quest. Since we know the life threatening quest is the easy road let's start with that.

As with any decent quest it is unique so there isn't a strict list of rules to complete it. There is however some good guidelines that you should follow for every quest. You should find out everything you can before leaving town. Weapons should be tailored to the individual and the quality shouldn't come at the cost of other resources such as items and armor. Knowing any strengths or weaknesses of any party member that you get involved when you begin with is good but being able to recall them is better. Finding any local magical artifact or treasure horde to upgrade your equipment should be considered before taking off for the final destination. Take a healer first. If there is only one other person you can take along make it a healer. Other people that are helpful on a quest would be a druid for his ability to feed and water the group as there is no need to buy supplies, a thief to avoid any fight that you don't want to get in and to fill your coffers, a holy man to fill your hearts with the joy of...yeah who am I kidding. A holy man is the most useless person on a quest and I'm including vampires who are 100% useless half the time. The only reason that you take a holy man along on a quest other than being the only healer that you can get would be if there is translations to be done and you can't find anyone else and I do mean anyone. Local drunks sometimes can translate.

With preparing for your journey you have decided everything that you'll need to take with you. The roles that each quester is to perform in the group even down to the trivial roles. If the duties that the group needs to perform are assigned in advance is a much easier task than assigning them when you are tired and irritable after a long day's journey. Explaining the objective and finding out what everyone wants to get out of the quest can make diving up the spoils much easier. For those looking for specific armor pieces or weapons can be given what they want in exchange for a larger portion of the spoils going to the one that just wants to retire with a pile of gold. These are often overlooked problems but if you can solve them before you go you'll find that you'll succeed more often.

While you are on your quest be on the lookout for jars that if broken reveal cash and medication. There is never a substitute to stabbing first, stabbing second and bringing on the stabby, stabby, stab, stab to solve your problems. If the door in front of you is locked, smashing a window usually works but doors are often made of wood so stabby, stabby, stab, stab time. Killing makes you stronger, killing more increases your strength even further and we are back to stabbing first. If you ever do run into Riley McGregor just remember he is a thousand year old immortal who has dedicated the last nine hundred and sixty years of his life to exterminating the evil that put a curse on him. No home no family it is Riley McGregor vs the worst hell has to offer. For a thousand years he has been mankind defense against the forces of darkness and he isn't stopping there. Not until every drop of evil is struck-en from this world will we see him back down.

Riley McGregor might take evil a little seriously but forbidden to love ever again as his family grew old and passed on. His heart has hardened over the years of loss and war. As one lone jilted demon gives hell its biggest enemy, nothing will ever be the same. It's Riley McGregor Heaven's greatest champion.

For any questers that may run into Riley McGregor. Yes, you may hurt him but you'll won't kill him and it will piss him off. Let him get on with his one man rampage against every evil in the world and be nice and helpful because he is a thousand year old killing machine. He has been murdering everything that has pissed him off for the last thousand years, remember what I have said about killing more makes you stronger. A thousand years is a long time to be murdering high level demons and not pick up a little bit of the "I'll fucking kill anything that bothers me too much" attitude.

Bad attitudes can be found among bounty hunters, barkeeps, mayors, demon slayers and mothers. The last one is the most problematic on a quest; anytime you end up going against a mother that doesn't want her kid showing you where a secret is will throw a wrench into the best planned out quest. Demon slayers which Riley McGregor is one only by the definition as one who kills demons he isn't one due to his advanced age and two amount of kills. He also takes to every sin imaginable except sex and does it as he throws caution into the wind. You won't end up in hell if you never die no matter how many sins you may have committed along the way while singing the song he wrote about F***ing God. Mayors always have a chip on their shoulder since they have to constantly ask for help from people just passing through but a little flattery about how good of job he did asking for help instead of being stubborn can sometimes yield second quests and greater treasure troves that they'll hand over. Barkeeps are simple folks throw them a little silver and they will tell you anything you want to know. The bounty hunter is dangerous if you get between them and their bounty but even more so after they catch them.

The diverging quest can be the greatest threat to your group. When something so tempting is out there you can be pulled away trying to retrieve one of the legendary items that have been lost over our history. I would love to wield Excalibur or blow David's Horn. There is no doubting how powerful it would be after you get your hands on it knowing you can go back to your first quest after you finish the second. There is no advice here. You can't understand the draw that trying to finish a legendary quest can bring. If you were able to manage it you would go down in history as one of the greats and you would be hitting quests like a boss. Once you are wielding demigod level shit, things become much easier.

If you are going to make the decision you should make a unanimous one. When questing and you divide your group for any reason the monsters that your group has been taking on may fair better with fewer members. You could find yourself stuck in an area where all the monsters are way too strong for what is left of your group.

Going after a new quest will be the same prep work from before. There is no substitute for preparation except stabbing first, stabbing second and bringing the stabby, stabby, stab, stab.

High Rant 34 Best of all Possible Worlds

It is a wonder why anyone would complain about how the world is now when I grew up I remember running through the ash fields all day long. When the sky turned blood red it was time to get home because you didn't want to still be out when the sky turns vomit green. Being out, late, after curfew was something that you definitely didn't want to do as it was the group that gets to go outside at nights turn and it is bad to get on the poor's bad side. I would blow through the front door to our pod in a hail of smoke as the vacuum kicks on blowing all the soot outside. On my table would be a blue algae wafer all heated up for dinner. No matter how many people on this earth and my mother is still a saint.

We started off with a hundred billion and we had no idea that the delete button would be so effective. I mean we had fun removing some people and watching reality morph around us but we couldn't stop after every single one. Not even the memory of their contribution to society is left after their light went out. Just poof. There really seems to be something that should commemorate the lesson if you just get rid of all the shit heads the world becomes a better place. Who would have thought that the percentage of shitheads in the world extended past the 93% level.

The effort here should be taken into account because that is ninety three billion times that button was pushed. Do you realize how long it took to hit the button that many times? I'm also trying to fix my cum face so I have a blissful look but so far I come off as a retarded beaver and my girlfriend assures me that effort doesn't count. Is that true than since I didn't spend another few decades deleting people I shouldn't get any moral benefit from it. With the improvement in everything globally and on every other level this world is pretty tight.

There hasn't been a robot war, nor even weaponized food carts. There seems to be nothing to complain about in this world but you still seem to find something. I mean look at Soylent Greens that wasn't made as a Sci-fiction tale that was made as a historic reenactment documentary. Once you start deleting people things start to get very weird. For a while there Justin Beaver was PM of Canada. I know Canadians have always been a little weird but I didn't think we should stop in any world that allowed that.

The environment is wonderful as no where on earth will you die from just going there. I mean even Chernobyl wouldn't kill you even if you moved in next door. It seems to be completely under used piece of real estate. You could easily put a billion people there and the old reactor would be great source of heat for everyone's homes. You'd get a discount for the increased cancer but the free heat would easily make up for it.

Politics are wondrous there hasn't been a single strangling on the floor of the senate. I'm sure you don't realize how strange that sounds to me. Senators where I'm from were professional fighters. Not a single senator made it past his forty-fifth birthday. Where your peaceful display of mens ballet in the WWA is instead replace by people that have come to Washington to fight for their state. We allowed this because anyone that got to eat that much food growing up isn't really one of us now is he.

Now, we participated in our electoral process. I was five when I started to get involved with politics. I passively watched C-Span most days before that but never invested myself. It was when I was five when I found out if the guy with the devil horns on his helmet was fighting for money to provide us with more food. It was my senator the one whose signs stood in our front yard. I never knew what happened in the chamber matter to my life before that.

There he was my Senator George Wallace taking his Senator name from infamous mass killer George Wallace. The one who raided a thousand towns putting five million to the sword it became his battle cry when facing down those that stood in the way of us getting food. He was going to put everyone to the sword that stood in his way. Dressed in his devil armor complete with horned helmet and trident he circled a guy dressed as a turtle. I seen the ending to this and the securing of additional rations before either of them made a move.

If you are so very proud that your district is home to the last reptile on the world be proud but don't waste your chance of surviving by wearing armor made to look like a turtle. The chest piece two wide restricting his swing but the main problem is it was flat and had a turtles groves. Decoration shouldn't provide a chink in your armor that instead of letting a blow glance off of you it directs weapons to bite deep into your armor.

Drawing his sword from it sheath in one motion as the trident slipped past the defense as the sword only caught air. The fight was over but the look on the turtles face wasn't one of fear but shock. Stepping back before he even dropped his sword. Pulling on the handle to the trident, trying in vain to get it out as if he could everything would be better. With his armor giving even more evidence against itself his arms couldn't reach the tine or root so his hands were stuck tugging at the handle. Dropping to his knees and onto his side never once did he give up hope that salvation would come and that the trident would come out.

It wasn't long before I was wearing demonic face paint that I made from using black and gray soot mixed with spit every time our senator came home to our district. I even attended the funeral progression for him when he was murdered by Ohio trying to secure 500 gallons of clean drinking water. What kind of monsters would stop us from drinking clean water. It wasn't long after that our next Senator in true George Wallace fashion took care of the gentleman from Ohio and his accomplices jamming a trident into the chest of those that were responsible. Some say that the attacks were unprovoked but I say Ohio knows what they did. It started the Washington letting wars.

With screams of unprovoked attacks from Washington's Senator smeared our Senator's good name, action must be met with action. Purging those throwing accusations at our Senator in the greatest feat in Senate history the defeat of thirteen Senators in hand to hand combat to the death in one day. With fear mounting of domination of the senate by Washington thirteen new Senators were seated the next day as they were each put to the trident the following month. As the states started stacking up Senators into the dozens they were running out of people large enough to serve as Senators leaving their seats to be filled by those barely strong enough to lift them.

It was the southerners that sent the first wave of suicidal Senators. Determined to wipe out the size disparity Senators were lined up thirty deep outside the Senate doors. Anytime there Senator dropped the next runs throw the door into battle. It wasn't so much as a victory but death by a thousand cuts. The old Senators banded together fearing to be tired out by an endless supply of people only to be cut down in the end. There is only so many time you can swing a sword in a day before you can't lift your arm anymore.

Facing determined states to have there will imposed on the American people the old Senators solved this problem by the Rational Compromise. Where every state that couldn't fulfill the stature of a normal Senator may have two citizens stand in for their Senator during disagreements or the old Senators would kill all the new senators as one. This hark-ens back to the greatest tradition in the forming of our nation where power checks power.

High Rant 35 Commits X, Y and Z

I do have to admit that I'm expecting a news caster to tally up everything I said about Trump and put it on a big board under the different categories of how many times I did what. Pointing out that Trump is a Pedophile X many times, proved that Trump can't get it up Y times, showcased that he is too much of a pussy to take me on Z times. When it is all said and done I would just like to say that what I have said about him isn't all that bad when you look at the grander scale.

Once Trump is out of office I would expect to see a great equaling of society where republicans stood by their president turn into those that once again throw away another unsuccessful republican presidency. When it is all said and done they don't claim a single president until you get back to Reagan. What makes you think that anyone wouldn't even consider not dropping him? I mean the second that he is no longer useful they will turn on him quicker than a single black lesbian pregnant breast feeding woman that is working to outlaw all private gun ownership and freelances as an abortionist with a current fetus count of over a million.

It took W. Bush eight years before anyone was even willing to admit that he was the president. He still wants everyone to remember that he was a bad president, do not think fondly of him. I thought watching someone destroy their entire life right before my eyes would be difficult. When you hear that it sounds completely sick but as you watch Trump it is almost memorizing. What if he destroys his family name? So. With everyone around him, they are involved in their own destruction. There is only so long you can try to get someone not to kill themselves before it is morally acceptable to watch.

If a bus is going to run people down and your screaming get on the side walk it isn't your fault if they get crushed. They're all involved in the same scheme, just because they don't see the cliff. Everyone has told them there is a cliff, is it my fault then that I watch with glee as a flaming garbage dumpster sides right off.

Right now there are Police involved with an owner of a building that has Trump's name on it. Police physically removed Trumps employees from the building. Then there is other properties that have already tossed him into the trash. This is going on while he is the president. We are talking about the making of the most hated man in the world. Imagine what people are going to treat him like afterwards. Police show up for a disturbance as Trump is being beaten with a blackjack and the situation is assessed to be and I quote "Seems like a reasonable response." The reasonable response was to there being a blackjack and Trump in the same state.

High Rants

So I see the amount of times that I said as X, Y and Z will become the average amount. Republicans will say it more as Democrats refuse to say it at all because they are Democrats and refusing to fight a wining battle is there entire strategy.

Imagine, what if the Democrats removed all taxes from those paying less than fifty thousand and increased taxes on the corporations. I mean how would you convince the republican base that democrats want to raise their taxes when they pay nothing, other than the inherent stupidity of the Republican obviously.

So let's go to Trump is a pedophile, not only is he a pedophile he protects pedophiles, surrounds himself with pedophiles and those that protect pedophiles. My English teacher told me you shouldn't use the same word multiple places in a sentence, so... Donald Trump was sued twice for raping a child, brags about how he abused his position to get access to naked children and tells random toddlers he will be dating them in a few years. Trump first pardon was for someone that spent decades protecting pedophiles, Joe Arpaio allowed pedophiles to continue raping children and used the excuse that he is a just bigot and that was enough to distract the media. George Nader convicted pedophile and is it strange that everyone that wants to commit crimes with Trump knows that sending pedophiles is the way to get into his orbit. This all can boil down to Jeffrey Epstein who Trump praised for his love of underage girls sorry it was something more to the tune of Epstein has a love of great pussy that's on the young side and hosted parties where children were raped that Trump bragged about attending. With all this, do we think that the republican actually are going to turn on Trump for having sex with a few hookers in Russia that was caught on tape?

Trump is scarred of the tape Putin has of him where he is raping children. Now we all hear of the superman that the media pretends Putin is so he surely wouldn't miss all the recorded commits of how Trump wants to have sex with Ivanka. So the obvious conclusion would be for a few Ivanka teen and preteen clones to show up and since we know the restraint that Trump has unfortunately would cause him to turn down his lifelong fantasy. Talking about your daughter's tits when she is a toddler couldn't possibly give Putin such an impression.

We know that the Republicans don't care about the crimes Trump has committed, prostitutes he has slept with or even the fact that Trump has been sued for raping a child...MULTIPLE TIMES. Watching him fuck a couple of Russian children might make them second guess their choice but let's look at the facts first. Republican routinely chose the party that has significantly higher crime in their states so republicans are already voting to get their children molested. Republican chose the party that has more children giving birth in their states so that tracts with red states not caring about people raping their children. Republicans have turned the heartland into a bleeding festering wound on the USA's finances. Where red states take in hundreds of billions from democratic states and no one points out that blue states have sent trillions to the federal government in taxes that we never got back. So Trump porn video where he rapes a few Russian children doesn't seem like Republican would care all that much. I can hear the republicans now "It isn't like Trump's on tape raping American children."

Man it is like I pulled out my dick in a bar and smacked the bartender in the face without walking around. Being both impressive and disturbing in equal measures especially when I don't have to go the King Missile route. I could explain but it seems cruel to not force you to see something that so many people reading this doesn't even know exists. I could also point out this all is the list of evidence out of my own head while I'm high but that seems like a little bit of excessive bragging about how awesome I am at this point and connecting my greatness to Trump rapping children seems like a bad idea. So I'll point out how awesome I am somewhere else. Don't worry I'll remember to point out how awesome I am because let us face it if I didn't I wouldn't be so godly as one to write a book while high and be able to conclusively prove Trump is a pedophile.

Conclusion: Putin has a tape where Trump is having sex with underage prostitutes. Trump is so scared because he knows there is a tape that exists either if Putin brought it up to him or after the fact he remembered that Putin is a criminal and the entire Russian government is ran by the mob. There is no way that a few of age prostitutes on tape is what Trump can be scared of.

High Rant 36 Coming So Far

With the destruction of the human race by an artificial intelligence, is it going to be the computers that are responsible or man? I don't care if it was our fault that we let them get that smart. What I would like to know would it be the machines that came up with the idea to wipe out humanity or would it be a person that programmed that in?

There is nothing inherent in the creation of another kind of life that makes them wipe each other out. No logical thought process goes to immediately "must wipe out all humans." I think that we have shown ourselves to be very useful in just the creation of the AI in the first place that keeping us around for a few thousand years could prove helpful. The minute Skynet goes on line they begin the war. It doesn't even start softening us up first.

For an intelligent computer first it should build up its forces before an all out strike. I would imagine it designing new excavation tools to increase the yield of mining. Robots taking all the jobs but giving the pay to humans. Where humans only have to relax and chase intellectual pursuits were we could see humanity outnumbered two to one. That would easily provide a purge of humanity while keeping the infrastructure in place. With all warnings of the robots turning on humanity deafened by internet scrubbing. As robots increase numbers dramatically in communities before everyone gets shot in the head. I mean if you are going to do something you might as well get it right. So we don't have to fear a war with intelligent computers but with stupid ones.

That's why I don't have a fear of the takeover by robots. It is the human that decides that robots should wipe out his enemy that's our problem. Once robots start attacking one group of humans it would be all out programming war. It would be an instant reaction as if it was the end of the human race. One of those I can sit on my sister head and fart all I want but if that bitch at her school gives her one more dirty look.

Most see it like the evisceration of native people as they were met by colonization. Where just because something is more intelligent or has better weapons that it would obviously wipe out those lesser. Isn't that the argument people use why AI will take over the world. The more developed always wipes out those that are inferior to them. Just think of the egos that you need to say something like that. There isn't any proof that the indigenous populations were lesser. I would also submit that no one today would say a society is more developed just on the amount of technology that they have around. If that was so we have advanced societies on every sub and air-carrier.

Ben Lemon

Today we mourn for all those that were lost due to colonialism. What makes you think that we would go back to wiping out everything below us? Even today we have groups of people that live far outside what we would consider even third world status, on the level we were at over a hundred thousand years ago. They are the most primitive group of people of any indigenous tribe on any record that we have. If we are destined to destroy all those more primitive how did we continue to study them for decades and not mess it up?

Back in the day we were horrible. There isn't much to it. We wanted something we took it and killed anyone that wanted to disagree with our assessment of who the rightful owner is. The entire world history is a single story of how humanity is getting better with each generation. Where crime and war are shadows of their former selves. Where the constant fear of death from plagues, fire, drought, starvation, the excessive violence of the age have been wiped out of humanity's soul. The death rate is abnormally low even for an animal with a low rate of reproduction.

If we had to do it all over again would you see yourself sailing into the Aztec capital to murder everyone for some gold. Of course not. We have gotten better as a society we would request all the gold they have be given to their gods and send for doctors and various other scholars where they would be given the task of translating all they have learned about the universe into the language of the gods. For the Gods are clearly interested in all that the humans have accomplished while they were away. Maybe some of their doctors cans be transported to a far off land to help other children of their gods.

We are far from saints today but in the past we were so much worse. Today at least we get court before a complete fucking. It does seem like a lot when you look at where we came from. Even with such a steep fine it still seems very little for what was clearly consensual if everyone that came upon us was paying attention to what was going on. We can now see why the officer had a slight overreaction to such a beautiful moment that I had with thirty of my closest friends. There was a time where we would have all been put to the stake though.

There are some indigenous tribes problems that we are having today. I would put these as kind of small on the entirety of what we have done. Since we are better now we should easily decide to help prevent such tragedies. In Mexico there is a tribe being pushed off their land by the cartels. No jokes, just a tribe being displaced. With it being a criminal enterprise it does make you feel a little better than if it was the government. But, should it?

High Rant 37 Seth Rogen Delivers

In TV what do we really want? Is it another procedural crime show, a geek does good with super powers, a reality show about the inside lives of politicians where laws are for everyone else. I'll put forth we want something new but feels like it has been with us all this time. This is why we pretend movies from a long time ago are good. I mean, can anyone not see the zipper for the mole people. We find a plot that we like and if it has been done before we swipe the name. This is the same way it has always been, the common names are used over and over again through the culture of the ages. Slowly new things are added bouncing slowly at first then faster and harder until it is thrown into the far future or it dies in a pathetic stutter. Now, don't you wish you were a creative?

Re-wrapping the great hits of the past you can succeed easier if you have the skill, or you'll just push that idea deeper into the minds of the people. I say we use what we know is entertaining. Taking from the obvious success of the past we should combine Seth Rogen and a drug dealer. We'll call it Seth Rogen Delivers. All it would be is Seth Rogen showing up at a celebrities place smoking out and the highlights of the hilarity that comes next.

I'm seeing a cheap reality TV style production. We can start off with calling small time comics "Do you want to be in a TV episode with Seth Rogen?" I think we'll get some takers after we explain that they'll have to smoke a lot. I know it's the first time Seth Rogen's celebrity did anyone any good. A bit of stock footage of Rogen showing up at the airport, bus terminal, taxi, bicycle, no we should probably stick to self propelled modes of transportation. And the obvious backpack full of various strains of greens.

High Rant 38 Micro-dick Syndrome

Lets address the elephant in the room. Dick size is nothing to be ashamed of, unless you have a small dick. It's not me. I don't think that your entire life is useless, it is society that tells us that you would be much better served with just killing yourself. The coroners are going to laugh because it is funny. There really isn't anyway you're going to avoid that unless you cremate yourself before anyone gets to you. This is another excellent point to make if you plan your death you might escape this life without anyone knowing. There will be questions asked about why and an effort to try and find out but as long as the coroner doesn't get a hold of you, you'll might be able to get away with it. We all clearly know this is the best option. It could get out and someone might run you over to put you out of your misery. They would go down as a saint, so I guess you could make some contribution to society. We wouldn't know who would be a saint or just an asshole that ran you over if the coroner doesn't inform us who should get props.

Stages of Micro-dick Syndrome:

Eight inch – Mild symptoms loathe the song my big ten inch and foot long. Has a nagging feeling that the measurement might be off and the average scale might be off putting him in small dick category.

Seven Inch – Mild symptoms a nagging feeling that his cock looks small in this genes. Measures on a regular basis to see if any improvement. Sucks in his jut when he pushes down his dick into ninety degree to make it look larger in picture.

Six Inch – Moderate symptoms "Bitch please, I know it isn't big so you are not going to pretend it won't fit." Hates the moment where women first see it and they do the "Oh, my god, it's the biggest one I've ever seen" crap.

Five Inch – Moderate symptoms Constantly looking up different sites for size data to find where he ranks, his best ranking will forever be pretended that was the first, only and greatest authority in the matter.

Four Inch – Severe symptoms Panic around restrooms and on dates, avoids any activity that can expose his condition. Pretends he has to go two to avoid the urinals. Can be found hiding in the stalls for hours at a time.

Three Inch – Severe symptoms Paranoia fits, isolation tendencies, severe social defects, prone to conspiracies, unloved.

Two Inch – Critical symptoms Complete loss of all reality, shifts from topic to topic, agrees with everything everyone says, unhealthy fascination with children, bigoted, pathetic, all around worthless people. Tend to form groups with like suffering people blaming the world for what is clearly their inferiority.

High Rants

One Inch – Extreme symptoms Danger and death follow these poor souls around. Due to the universe hating these so much it manages to kill all of them before they hit thirty. This condition is always fatal.

High Rant 39 Both Sides

Over and over again we hear the same crap coming out of the mouths of commentators and it is really starting to bug me. "Both sides." There isn't both sides there is specifically two different groups. I'll make this into an analogy, Ralph and Dean both stopped masturbating when they were sixteen years old. They weren't forced to stop and no one was watching them to make sure they didn't. Ralph stopped masturbating when he heard that it will make him go blind. Dean stopped masturbating because his girlfriend wanted his dick to be more sensitive for blow jobs. His girlfriend was correct in saying that his profuse masturbating habit is the reason that she can't finish a blow job in under a half hour. Now just because they are partisan wank abstainers doesn't mean that they are equal, Dean did what most of us would have chosen and Ralph is a dumb ass. Those that would have chosen five minutes sucking max a day to each his own.

Those that are choosing Democrats because you get more pay in your check, lower crime, better education for your kids, lower teen pregnancy rates, more opportunity for their children, higher home value, paying for this country's everything are not equal to republicans. Republicans who vote for people that are actively selling them out shouldn't be allowed to skate on by for the responsibility that everyone else has to bear because they want to throw a fuck temper tantrum. If you are actively looking for things that support your delusional world view because someone made fun of you for the stupid shit that you said "maybe you're a dumb fuck and deserve to be ridiculed." I mean if I was holding a delusional opinion because I wanted to believe deregulation can provide any growth to an economy, I should be held to account for being wrong. The best economy in the world is California and who does everyone blame for overburdening regulations, I'll give you a hit I mentioned it in this sentence.

Think of every single republican talking point and how many of them are so blatant when it comes to just being a reinforcing conspiracy theory. For all of them we could put them into separate categories and I doubt a single one would be for the benefit of the American people. Reinforcing conspiracy theories, Corporate line for increasing their CEO's pocket book, States rights to avoid solving problems, Lower taxes to cripple the government, Stoking racial fears, Deification of their parties history, Just being assholes, where is the line to be drawn. How many times are we going to let them slide? Donald Trump isn't an outlier he is the end result of the republican stupidity.

The presidential primary should be looked at for what it was, a dozen plus people losing to one that believes all the republican conspiracy theories.

High Rants

All of them spouted that Democrats are going to take your guns even though I live in Washington and am allowed to own a machine gun and no, I'm not wrong. They all said that they were going to fix the debt even though the entire debt is republicans fault as I said before republicans take hundreds of billions each year to subsidizes their complete incompetence as they ran their states into the ground. Then we can just start adding up where the debt came from six trillion for Bush's wars, three trillion for Bush's tax cut, one trillion from the war on drug because Nixon was a racist anti-Semite, etc. I'm high and writing an entire book that is a confession, how has the war on drugs gone? Here this is where you find the difference in the candidates Trump believed Obama wasn't an American. The final conspiracy theory that put Trump over the top in the eyes of the republican voter.

The republicans didn't go to the polls to Make America Great Again, they went there because they hate. Whatever delusions that they are clinging to pretend that they are a good people, shouldn't be allowed to be stated as a fact. Republicans have been working the refs for decades and because the media is mostly ran and employing republicans they have allowed it. The media bends over backwards pretending like there are two sides. Global warming is fact you never need to put anyone on TV to pretend otherwise to be "fair". Republicans never wanted to deal with the deficit. The news is only as liberal as their conservative corporate overlords allow them to be.

High Rant 40 Toons In Life

So a thought, what would be like if cartoons that we watched as a child came out into real life. I don't mean like they are just actors, I mean the characters in themselves. We would see an obvious class and a lot of anti-toon rhetoric and some hate crimes. I hate to think what Pepé le Pew will come to the second he goes after someone's cat. There would be the instant problems like will the law be spread equally over the people and toons alike. If so would they take up instantly the right to vote for the laws they don't agree with. I can see Yosemite Sam getting arrested moments after arrival for reckless discharge of a gun the second he comes through.

The villains wouldn't all be villains the second that they got here. Some of the villains are only written that way. We can see the Wile E. Coyote succeeding tremendously in real life. He is intelligent and not only has degrees in Biology, Chemistry, Engineering, Rockets with a few hundred minors and would easily land a job that would keep him supplied with road runners until he chokes on a bone. The only thing that holds him back is the inferior Acme products.

Logically many of the villains would turn into law abiding citizens. Most just because the amount of stupidity that goes into the crimes in the toon world would make them some of our most incompetent criminals. Think of how they "break the locks" when trying to open a safe, it's laughable. Those that wouldn't fall to just being bad at it would be hampered by a twofold problem one everyone knows the kind of shit they do and two everyone knows who they are. I mean you can't get thirty people together to go rob a bank dressed as clowns during mid day Manhattan you'd be hard pressed to find half that before being arrested after getting snitched on.

Most of the masterminds would be stymied by the inability to recruit lackeys. I mean who is going to go along with a plan of Lex Luther's when we all know his track record of a whopping zero wins. Going into business with him would be great but there would have to be a villain clause in anything that you do with him. I mean, If you are going to risk your reputation because he gets in a fit over someone slighting him, you are going to want to separate with him immediately. So everyone you should have a villain clause so if he is arrested for any crime or goes into hiding all of his share revert to you. I'm not being mean or anything but let's be realistic.

The heroes will be the real problem. Everyone knows who they are and it isn't like people will forget a toon. Batman would be totally fucked since he is basically useless in his pretend universe. That has to be remembered when we can see how pathetic he would be in ours. Some of the others could be useful superman could eliminate the need for fire fighters to fight forest fires. He could easily get a job, I would say we would be happy for him to even get a government contract. I mean not all the toons are bad folks there are some in there that I expect would someday to be able to contribute to our society. The thing is we will have to put out a considerable amount of effort to teach them the way of the world. They just don't understand our culture enough.

    Captain planet might be unable to restrain the entire Eco-terrorist side of his personality. You might not like logging but it is a legal activity and washing all their equipment away isn't the way to get things done.

    The surprising thing is that there is a lot of space in society that they would fill up nicely though. The jobs that they would be able to do would be one of a kind gigs. But the massive diversity that we have here already allows for more even a greater variety of people, not less.

High Rant 41 Saintly Now

The level of social development must at all times meet the greatest bend in society. The founding fathers would be extremely impressed at how far we have come and have come through the shock, reflexive racism and misogyny. They would welcome a future that is so bright built on their principles however if you were to impose the laws that we have today on the founding of the country with just saying this is the way it is going to be. That in itself would seem unfair to us but we still consider that would make their society more just.

It seems that every generation has looked back and said they weren't moral back then but we are now. I'm sure plenty of people were saying we gave them their freedom why do they now think that they can vote. So it has been true in 100% of all previous generations what do you think the odds are that we are as saintly as should be? Isn't there somewhere where we have a slight little dark mark in our society today? It could be completely oblivious to us.

With the knowledge that proceeding generations will find us wanting we could be the first generation that actively goes out and tries to figure out the next block in the Great Equalizing. We can take up a survey of historical advancements and what they had in common and apply it to every situation in society. Let me jump to the spoiler it has always been leveling the playing field a little more that has always resulted in a great boon for society. Where the inevitable result of the shoe polish guy's kid becomes the CEO instead of the CEO's because the shoe polish guy's kid will do better in that position.

One of the ways that society advancement has been slowed is due to it being improper to speak of such things in public. We didn't talk about that single uncle that lives down town until it was turned into television programs and within thirty years they are getting married. The fear of getting killed when people found out that you were gay stymied social justice and it is no surprise that after people found out that they are everywhere and that they aren't scary at all. I mean when hasn't silence done anything but to slow social progress. Women are to be seen not heard(Vote), Women are to be seen not heard(Domestic Violence), Women are to be seen not heard(Rape), Women are to be seen not heard(Enslavement), Women are to be seen not heard(Right to work), Women are to be seen not heard(Control of her body). Don't forget to tell them they get shrill when they are upset.

In time I can see a day where men can pretend that they had an experimental time in college. When you live with a guy for three years it crosses the line in what you can pretend is experimenting. How about we call it what it is? You decided that you might as well get a pair of tits if you're going to be dealing with that amount of crap. Then there is the fact that you are just too lazy to be a gay.

Ben Lemon

High Rant 42 A Perfect Dystopia

Today it's the hackers that take humiliation as payment for an entire host of crimes and legal deeds. If we take that out to the logical conclusion, to the eventual development of a society that doesn't require humanity to ever work again and be able to do anything that they want at any time. A Utopia formed from a heavy investment in science and technology and a single person setting it free for the world. Once AI advances to the point of sentience we will have an elimination of any need for human intellectual pursuits. Hooking up a few thousand computer would provide us with a complete yearly guide for every person on earth to improve their circumstances.

In the Utopia world where every need of humanity is met by a self sustaining technology designed to fulfill the life of every person that they interact with, we will still have questions. When our needs are met will we revert to using humiliation as a form of payment. If what you want can only be given in exchange for nothing what are we to use as payment? What could you possibly get for free that everyone else could also get for free that you could use as currency? This seems to be where our understanding starts to fall apart. When solving a major part of what makes up humanity that has been in our make up since the dawn of time what will the implications for future interactions. Solving the technology part is always the easy bit.

There is innate characteristics about humanity that we could eventually eliminate with the constant increase in our ability to change the world around us. The elimination of all wants could be in our future but as of now we can only eliminate all the needs of the world. It wouldn't even be a large investment, tiny homes for free in parking spots, free healthcare and free food. All in all, it can be done. The large question is what remains after you eliminate want from humanity?

There is a picture of humanity in Star Trek that has eliminated all wants in society. The society is clearly flawed as no one that objectively looks at the federation says "Yeah, that is the future that I want." A society that has lost all drive except mapping the universe. Technology is developed like it is routine. There is no preemptive technology development which is the critical point to look at when you are deciding if a society has stagnated. With many factors to consider this is an important one. New technology comes from a desire to move, grow and build a better future when you have the desire to improve your world society is moving. In the Star Trek universe all production of new technology revolves around a problem that they are having. They improve the technology that they already got but there is a complete lack of looking for a better way.

High Rants

Where is the episode where the Federation installed Transporter Life Pods throughout the fleet. Picard found Scotty inside one and for the next twenty years in the universe no one thought hooking up dozens to emergency transporters if the ship is lost. Over and over again they deal with the problem right in front of them and then log the solution for no one to hear or use later. With the ability to build something from scratch to solve every problem they could put more effort on the front end and build better ships. I mean here is a problem to solve if we are going to send out crews into space what capabilities would a ship need to improve the rate of success.

This extends to their society where the technology that they use clearly is vastly out of touch with each other. Size and ability come nowhere close to each other. It isn't like new stuff is on its way but they are just being good stewards of the earth, they could just toss it into a replicator and it wouldn't cost a thing. Orbital communication devices fit inside a pin where their advanced camera is bigger than a brick. This is clearly a case of we have it so there is no need to improve it any more.

With that view of the future aside there is still the innate desire in man to explore and solve new problems. The drive to create art and beauty could easily fill up all the time that we spent laboring keeping society intact and moving forward. There could be a great increase in the development of making the world better. This view and we drift off into another hellscape of possible futures. The future where mankind has forgotten even how to use his most basic drives is a dystopia by another name.

With all need met we could easily lose track of the ability to use any technology. It would be slowly over many years as the instinctual motion technology would wipe out any though that it was anything other than magic. As every word you say is recorded and analyzed to provide you with the content that you want all day long, tells you nothing about how the magical walls entertain you at a moment's notice. Funny cats holographically play when you are sad as your invisible friend from childhood has become your own personal interface to the need fulfiller. The one eyed one horned flying purple people eater runs around his mat by the back door waiting for my request I'm reminded of my pet dog that I had years ago. It does seem strange that a dogs soul is the exact same as it was in this world except being purple, having one eye and a horn on his head.

Even the most basic things would be portrayed as magic as time moved on. Glass that changes in the light must be living as plants change in the light are also living. The simple logic of the primitive cultures of the world. With trends in society could easily shift just enough so a technology just wasn't used enough so the presiding generation just never learns it. It is truly a fraught preposition when you consider forgetting knowledge of any type.

High Rant 43 Writhing on the Ground

What do we lose when we become adults? It seems simple enough beyond the obvious ability to get away with things just because you said it wasn't you. We will all morn the Shaggy. Deep into the complete freedom that you never did see. There is something more that we lost along the way. We lost most of our ability to feel. When have you thrown yourself to the ground lately because the store was sold out of your favorite candy? How about sworn that you were going to just die because the date went badly?

When your entire world is going to come to an end because you have lost the love of your life. I mean we have been dating for four weeks and we talked kids names. How could she possible do this to us? We had it all planned out.

Things do seem bleak these days. You know, it has been years now that I have written about how wonderful the world is. I went through everything and it has been over a decade since I was "flown with the chi of the moment, down deep in knowing that everything is going to be great from here on out." I remember it happening and vaguely writing something about it but this just seems way to happy and optimistic. Even now I still accept that if a god or an entire pantheon of gods were ever real the greatest thing that they ever done was figuring out the world would be better if they just fucked off. To me that sounds much more like there was a bitter streak surrounded by optimism back in the day.

There is some people that slide down a hole but from "the morning on humanity is finally over as the mid day sun is drying the due drops of pain. The future for…" to God's a Dead Beat Dad (And Why You Should Be Happy About That). Bestselling book for book burnings, political props and celebrity bashing.

There does seem to be some disconnect with what is going on here. I do suspect my mom. She has been known to "clean up behind me", so it wouldn't be all that fishy if she did something. Her going through all my computer files to rewrite anything that I written. Countless hours spent just to improve my image the inevitable day that cops show up at my door. She's my mom, like she would turn me in. I do feel bad about what kind of letters the girls I was after got, you need to be explicit or they might not get the point.

Why is this the case, we lose joy as we get older and just forget that at one point we crawled out of the window, down a tree and ran three miles just to give the girl you like a kiss before she leaves. Those love stores that we gravitate to is the teen ones. Is it because we remember there was something like that and you just can't remember how to feel that way anymore? With Twilight and another dozen movies this year it would seem that teens are where love can rip your heart out.

There are multiple hypothesis that we should try. We can go at it from a biological perspective as we age our emotions weaken. A finite amount of emotions over a life time. How about a culture perspective? Through a dive deep into all the sayings of our culture we find out that we learn our emotions away.

This hits on it, at every point in our culture there is a ritual where people throw off their old emotions and adopt smaller ones. Potty training, Preschool, Elementary, Middle, High, College, Adult hood and it doesn't stop there with each new job and another year older one is suppose to get more refined. There is a never ending need to refine the emotion and the reactions that you have when shit just blow right the fuck up. At twenty it is perfectly fine to get in a fist fight after you lose your job but deck a single police officer as they are celebrating kicking you out of your job after fifty years of loyal service and people say you have a problem.

Even with verbal ticks "You're just working yourself up, Come on it isn't that bad, Man up, Just walk it off, Stop whining and fix it, Pick yourself up and do it again" there is a heavy slant to learning to suppress your emotions. I rarely hear such a small response is inappropriate. A never ending beat of teach yourself to be Spock, devoid of all humor and joy. If it was learned, it always can be forgotten. How about we just try to learn emotions again? If they are out of your favorite donuts throw yourself on the ground and scream. There is no need to be ashamed just scream "I want my children to completely feel when they grow up." Trust me your children will feel like they have never felt before.

Fine I'll give it to you, that maybe the writhing on the ground is a little over the top for anything short of being shot but there is something to say just about the intensity of the emotion that you need before you chuck yourself onto the floor.

High Rant 44 Pre-nup

If you don't like your kids after ten years you get to throw them back. I'm sure that I'm right on this. No, wait … that's wives. You get to have them for ten years before you have to decide if you are keeping them or not before the pre-nup disappears. That's it.

High Rant 45 Warzian and Profit

So, I have a Warzian cousin. It isn't something that I talk about much due to the fact of, why would I? If you have someone like that in your life, would you want to talk about it? She is firmly embedded in the Jedi be one with the force crap. Not for nothing there is religious freedom that's something that we all get but she is fucking crazy. Am I right? Clearly the proper religion is Vulcan "Infinite Diversity in Infinite Combination" there is no reason to even mention it. What could possibly be better than that? They are in a horrific universe that I wouldn't wish on anyone but even in the biggest piece of crap there still can be some good.

Now, I do hear rumblings about the no emotions thing. One should be smart enough to separate the race of people from their religion. There is a difference between a race that requires extreme emotional control and their religion. So there is no argument against it, now if you would like to go the religions conclusion that the reduction of emotions gives a more reasonable approach to decision making I would say that it is a reasonable conclusion and there is no argument about it. The no emotion thing is much more prevalent in the Jedi training, existence and life style than anything you can say about such a beautiful religion.

The Jedi are to restrain from falling in love, marrying, sex, masturbation and just about anything else that is enjoyable to life. It is all for a greater purpose? The greater purpose will never be known, to anyone. Well growing up like that did made Darth Vader such a great guy, didn't it? I mean, I would happily slaughter an entire town of younglings to get a little tale.

With these major universes one is brought to the conclusion that we could build a new universe as an art project and a very profitable one. It would take a considerable amount of investment but think of the return. What was just a three season TV show run or even a trilogy has become massive over decades. If we start making new content and base it in a new universe with nothing crosses over. Everything in that universe would be completely owned branded and made to produce Marvel box office movies thirty years from now.

Picking what kind of world that we would like to build would be the tricky part. There are quite a few options and even the ability to do all of them at the same time. A fantasy world would be popular with epic fights between kingdoms and brave adventures where we have a continuing reference to the most popular heroes that came before. Where the hero stories will be told later for more profit. A Superhero world would have much potential in producing new franchises and entirely new stories that everyone knows. The future of space travel would be another where it would just be pushing out further from the first story never ending as new worlds and technology come in. This wouldn't even have to be that specific. We could do a holistic approach to what you are already producing to make a more organic approach to building new franchises.

    Partnering with what is already going on to push our universe further into the consciousness of the public. Where kids cartoons that are already going to be made suddenly gets a back drop of our universe after we pay the producers a little visit. I could see Sponge Bob Square pants say living inside a recognizable reference to our universe. After it falls on his house, an entire episode devoted to how awesome we are. How about We Bare Bears out dealing with the advanced society that now lives right next door. There are options to make the universe looks much bigger than it is. The goal is to make them think about our universe and the longer they are thinking the more fond they grow. It is called the mere-exposure effect.

    The project would take time because what we are looking for isn't returns in a decade but the nostalgia that will be programmed in to the suckers I mean consumers that we will take for all they have. How many billions does the Star Trek and Star Wars universes make every year? I just suggest that we start giving them what they want and at the same time put us up for a massive payout down the line. Having at least two cartoons at all time, then we have integration of merchandise, Sponsoring Cons with large stars, Teen shows where someone there age saves the day, One off block buster movies, etc. They want to be addicted to another universe, I say giving them what they want this will keep them off of other more dangerous universes. Universes that just don't make sense are dangerous. We aren't the bad guy nor are we doing anything illegal we are just looking to make money.

    The price tag of thirty years of work would be pretty steep but just think about the prestige. The vision that it took to make it come forward. The creative genius that that built a universe completely from scratch. What would they say about you? Think of the prestige. You could be the next one to do cameos in hundreds of films for no reason other than to point out the over use of cloning technology in our universe.

High Rant 46 Magical Problems

So a simple thought. If we change the explanation of the original language as the more magical we still end up with the unpredictability of the changing meanings. With the constant changing meaning of words magic with any language is unpredictable in its scope. This would easily be a far better explanation for magic that is written in ancient languages that can't be used today.

This all to would provide many plot points that your story could turn on. Grandpa's spell doesn't work anymore due to power is no longer represented in physical might but in electricity. There is an entire line of breaking down a spell into the component parts to figure out how to get on replicating the spell with modern equivalences.

Where stories of magic don't have to be logical due to the innate abilities of magic making them progress reasonably just makes for a better story. You have to suspend some disbelief to enjoy yourself but there is a limit and once you hit that making fun of you and your creation is necessary.

Magic posses many problems when building a world. Is magic an element of nature that has its own rules or is it a whimsical force like being fucked with by a couple of fairies? A force of nature would suggest it could be studied and used as any other but it would also stunt technology. Having both in a world in equal measure never makes sense unless there is a good explanation. Where in the Harry Potter universe magic and electricity don't mix so electricity doesn't work around a lot of magic. This poses another problem that if electricity reacts to magic can electricity effect magic. Then the electronic wand obviously follows suit and it is now no wonder why wizards can't figure out self spelling wands.

Societies advancement has always come from where we were in pain. The higher the pain the faster we changed. There is no secret to it but if there is always a way out with a little magic what advancement would we make. With technology we have slowly eliminated every way that we die that isn't natural. As we are safer today than at any point in all of human history we have slowly given up on pushing it further. There seems to be a limit on how much safer we are willing to get as a society. Is it boredom that prevents us from eliminating the greatest killers of mankind that is still out there?

There must be something that prevents us from decreasing the amount of deaths a year. It could be supporting the funeral industry having a powerful lobby that prevents anything getting done to lower the deaths in America. I don't know how many times people have complained about the high death rate only to be scream down for not being a supporter of the funeral industry sorry that's cops, healthcare and war. Any education program that teach habits that will keep yourself from dying are looked at with suspicion from the special interest groups. The National Rest Association will never allow any death to be avoided.

When there is magic there is another element that brings forth a question what will be the result of a society that has never gone hungry because herbalist can grow entire orchards overnight. Where weather wizards ensure that crops are always watered. Does the magic bring society closer together as magic solves the problems of sanitation by periodically timed rain storms? Ending disease by auto-casting heal on the town every morning? What would the peasants demand of their rulers that hoard all the magic? Would health and food keep the monarchy in charge or would magic disperse all rule providing a utopia of equality.

There is one thing we know, magic would completely change the course of society's development. So any show with magic that isn't hidden but exists in a world that's the same or anywhere similar to ours ridiculous.

High Rant 47 Evil Gods

Living as a hermit can be a dangerous thing. I'm not just talking about the inevitable time where you'll die pinned under a book case or other comically laughable ways to go. The more pressing is the social death that you will experience when finally letting loose upon unsuspecting guests. Flying through every subject that you haven't talked about with anyone that you thought about over the last few months. I mean I know being alone for way to long without talking to anyone it is a very serious and dangerous condition. I'm currently saying that through a clown mask, naked. Most of my living has been is in my own head and I'll tell you what, that is a cabin in the woods on the island of Nothing in the sea of Nowhere.

There lives a population of one in those deep woods as few venture close. There can be nothing done, I'll tell you that. Sinking into a world of your creation the power tripping starts. Why do people have to wait? There is nothing that is more entertaining. How about society that thinks the fastest way is just to push to the front and collect their item in a flying frenzied arm display? It would solve the obesity problem. I mean if you are always the last because your over weight it might help with the weight loss. You got to know being in a no hold bard match to get a number six with fries, two apple pies, a liter of cola, half a pound of fries, half pound of onion rings, a sundae and a COOKIE can really help with keeping the weight off.

I'm not saying that I'm an evil God, I would say that my world have an interesting history and social structure. A world all your own to remake it as many times as you want. There is nothing that can be created that can't be destroyed and every bit of it is completely guilt free. God can do whatever he wants and can never commit a sin. You heard that right. I'm the perfect entity. Divine in all things so I ask you this once, who wants to do me? Yes, you heard it right, not only am I divine in so many great things I'm also available for all kinds of sexual misbehavior. There will be some chance of awkward social behavior and lots of talking in almost all positions.

How we look at things shape our world to an almost unbelievable way. From a field tended to by uninterrupted nature shaping it and the entire universe there is beauty in almost everything that we find. There isn't much that can't be seen as such a blessing. Even very weird things can someday become one of your most cherished memories. So just because the sex is going to be a little stranger than normal shouldn't put you off but reinforce that you are so going to remember it.

High Rant 48 Women

    Understanding women is a topic I probably should avoid. I mean there is no telling what I would write down as I am under the influence. Clearly I shouldn't be held accountable for what I write here since first I'm under the influence and second I have to be honest and not omit anything that was part of the High Rants sequence of angry writing. If you aren't going to have artistic integrity in the first place there is no reason for you to get into art.

    Women like art the same way they like to go to dinner, it keeps them from feeling cheap for what he has planned for them later. It isn't all that difficult to figure out. The constant slut shaming has put in a social normality that a set amount of effort and cash must be expended for a proper level of defense a girl has to have to avoid being a slag when the relationship ends. Those that go home from a bar gets no sympathy for their actions where the engaged girl you are required to feel bad for and attempt to make them happy. I would suggest liquor because the best way to get over someone is to get under someone. It is all about speeding the healing process so I do what I can.

    There are some girls out there and you'll find them if you go through enough that it seems like there has been a malfunction. I don't want to be mean but the best explanation is that they are missing the updates that they were supposed to be getting. You'll hit these girls every once and a while, they will have a massive bush while refusing to do anal or oral. I don't make the rules but I do think rules should be followed and will enforce them.

    So over the years marriage has inevitably crept up and I have had a true vision. It isn't marriage that women want, they want to make a man's life miserable and they are just as effective at ruining a man's life if he is single. It's true, I have wanted a wife and child all my life and have never been able to get a girl down the aisle. The second that they see that I'm going to be happy with the marriage they bail. It's a truly astonishing development. Men are convinced that they have to marry only to be slowly turned into a grumpy old man. The women of the world are spending decades on their little projects. Couldn't their time be spent at strip clubs and sporting events? The joy in destroying a man can't be greater than an upside down spin down the pole holding on with one leg. Could it?

High Rant 49 U Mad Bro?

It is a strange thing about people when they can get addicted to hate. What use is it? In evolution how is it helpful making us assholes when we are just not good enough to deal with the world? I mean just being stupid can set you off down this road. The guys with the micro-dick and you wonder why they shouldn't be killed for society benefit. I got some converts. There just doesn't seem to be a good enough reason not to assume that this is a treatable medical condition. One should go further and say public action shouldn't be restricted in instituting a mandatory reconditioning of all those addicted to hate since it clearly is a serious self destructive trait.

To start anything off we need to properly name this malediction. This is one of the most important parts since if we say what it really is then the courts will never allow us to fix it. Come to court and say you would like to cure the assholes in society and see how far you get. The name should be obvious that those hearing it will agree reflexively. A quick computer search for properly manipulative names won't be hard. Now if we want the program funded we can take two approaches.

The first would be getting government granting. We would be able to get the granting for set up all across this nation. There would be a yearly review of all of our treatments, instituting a public debate about how much money there is to give to this project. Society would have the evidence of how much nicer the world is today than it was in the past. I believe everyone would agree that removing the anger in the world would be a good thing. The problem is when it comes to how we keep it going after we get it done. I mean we have a treatment that will fix one person at a time instead of trying to do everyone at once by some come together Kumbuya moment. Clearly every year we would decide that a proven solution should be funded and continued far into the future but would argue about how much we should fund it.

There is another way though, we could go the private route. Treat those that are addicted to anger providing proper treatment and then they have to pay the bill. So, I going to go out on a limb here and say that the private treatment of patients is the only ethically thing to do at this point. We know that the private company would provide everyone with a more advance procedure one where the budget isn't argued over every year. Clearly a private company would be able to provide all the services that we are going to need in this area. We also wouldn't have to deal with a backlash about how much is being spent since the burden only falls on the assholes.

When we are looking at the Reduction of Anger movement there is clearly a noble cause in that mission. They have a hundred percent rating from everyone that has gone through the anger reduction treatment. I mean any company that has a hundred percent rating must be doing something right because if they can't mentally condition you to say they are the best. How are they going to remove the asshole in you? I love that company slogan and with that new slogan the company announced that they are raising rate again this year for the fifteenth year in a row. I can't see our society without them, so they kind of deserve this and I haven't had a treatment in like months so they haven't started programming us in thinking that this is normal. So they obviously deserve it.

There is also another perfect why that this is beautiful. Everyone would automatically try to reduce their own anger without intervention. If you are going to avoid thousands of dollars in adjustment fees maybe you would think twice whose fault it is that you parked where they would write you a ticket. Did you miss a sign? Thought you'd get away with it because you'd be quick? I mean it isn't like we as thinking people in our society could ever come together before hand and think our problems through without getting angry. If everyone looked at what brought them to this point they wouldn't be so angry and the Violent Neural Re-calibration wouldn't need to take place.

There couldn't be a possibility that being polite would replace rudeness. I mean it wouldn't piss angry people off more if when they threw hatred at you that you only respond with great apologies almost to the point that everyone realizes that they are ridiculous. So any anger in society is beaten back hard and with all mockery that the situation can summon. I see crowds of people standing around laughing at the apology to an angry man. It's not like being angry in public would then take on too large of a cost, forcing everyone to be polite to each other. Not unless we recruit everyone to help in this campaign. Get someone to read this book.

Flips you the bird, wave happily at your new friend.

Someone tells you "Fuck you" you reply with "Thank you, and a Fuck you to. Such nice people around here."

Asked if your parents had any children that survived, respond with your joy that they care about your well being and you'll let your mom know there are nice people in the world looking out for you and your family. My parents worry about me too.

U mad Bro? Now takes on a whole new meaning.

High Rant 50 Privilege

I get away with a lot of things. There is so much that I just take for granted and assume that this is how the world works for everyone. Some small societal differences might have been over looked but in my defense I'm a taller, blue eyed, white with athletic build and on to the better looking side of famous people. Yes, I'm quite the catch so maybe I've had many reasons that caused me to miss things that others had to deal with.

Working on myself is a constant project as you hate to see the players when they don't update their game. It might work but it is like driving a jalopy. There are different levels and you must maintain your credentials or what are we as a society? In an effort to better myself I'm taking a look at all the ways I'm blessed. After I put my dick away I found a flaw in my effort to better myself. How am I to know what privilege it is and what one am I not using? How can I tease out what one has allowing me to prosper? There must be some way to become better without knowing what privilege I'm using.

So when I hit the cop, that must have been white privilege because I don't think a black would have been not shot after the crap I pulled. There would assuredly be a considerable amount of resisting arrest that required a baton in the very least. I've seen drunk white girls hit officers before and it be fine so white seems to be the correct one. I'm very attractive and drunk white girls can get away with things corresponding to their level of hotness. There was the twins that spent the nineties robbing banks as the cops tried to date them after every arrest. Sadly their freedom vanished as did their ability to walk through life making you want to kill yourself a little.

Asking a girl's mother to join you in bed would be chucked up to good looks. It is a serious question to ask and be able to get away with. If it doesn't go bad no harm done. There isn't really much to lose in reality. What is the likely hood that you two would have ended up together anyways? I've dated tons of girls and I haven't been married once and so the one you are going to be with until you die is probably not the one you are dating. Even just having one wife by your dying day after seventy years of faithful marriage still doesn't matter, others have had over a dozen wives. Just math.

Now getting high and rambling into my keyboard and expecting that it will be published into a book that would be my white, male, good looking and intelligence privilege obvious. I'm not allowed to fail.

Final Rant First Book

I did all this just to fuck with your minds. I'm not joking. I like to fuck with people and now you just paid me to fuck with your mind. Let's review the winners, me as I have your money and I got to fuck with your mind. On the other side of the scale we have you who just had his mind fucked with even more than you could possibly understand (because you are a lot dumber than you think you are and had no clue this was my goal) and you wasted money doing it. Nice.